150 SONGS WITH JUST 3 CHORDS

©Copyright 1999 Ekay Music, Inc., 2 Depot Plaza, Bedford Hills, New York 10507
Call Toll Free 1-800-527-6300
USA: musicbooksnow.com
Europe: goodmusic.co.uk

Table Of Contents

Arrangements By

Pete Dino
Marty Gold
Gail Masinda Hunt
Bill Irwin
Stuart Isacoff

Edited By

Julia Peña

A-Hunting We Will Go

TRADITIONAL

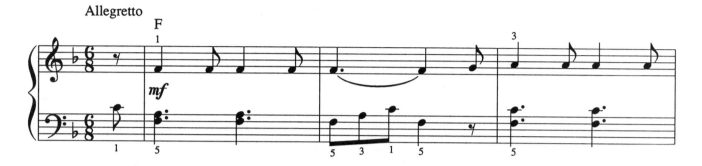

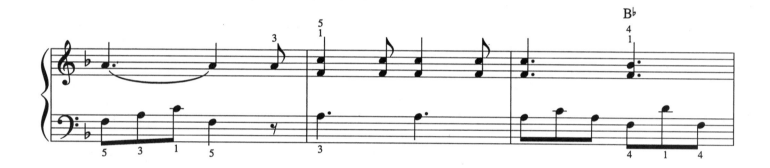

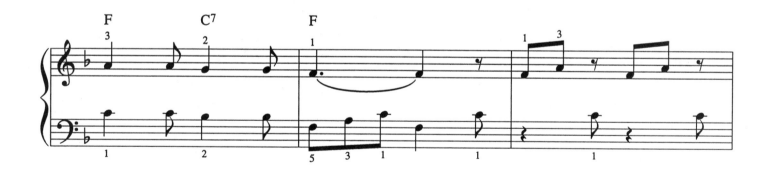

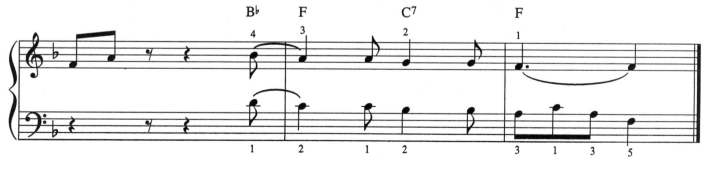

5

A-Tisket, A-Tasket

TRADITIONAL

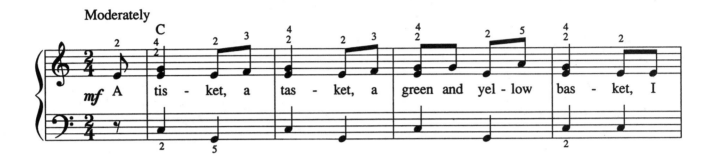

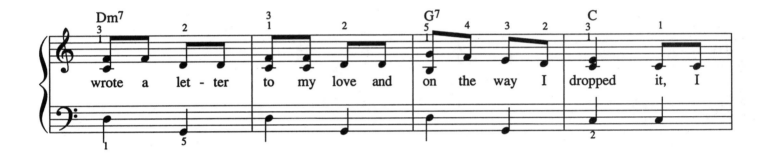

Ach, Du Lieber Augustin

Anonymous

Moderately

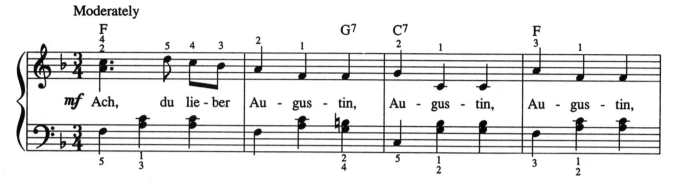

Ach, du lie-ber Au-gus-tin, Au-gus-tin, Au-gus-tin,

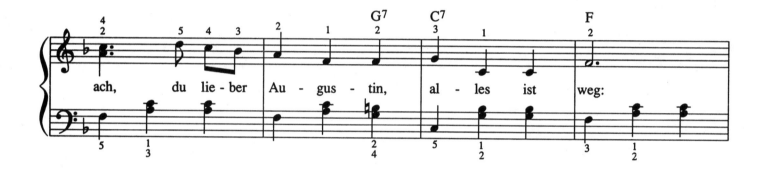

ach, du lie-ber Au-gus-tin, al-les ist weg:

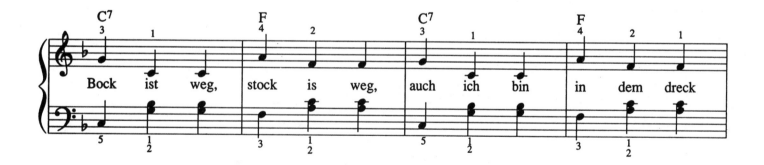

Bock ist weg, stock is weg, auch ich bin in dem dreck

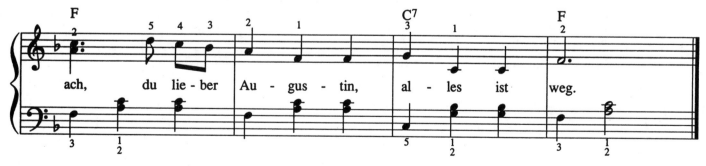

ach, du lie-ber Au-gus-tin, al-les ist weg.

Aloha Oe

Words and Music by
QUEEN LILIUOKALANI

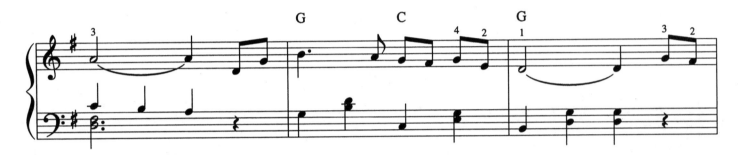

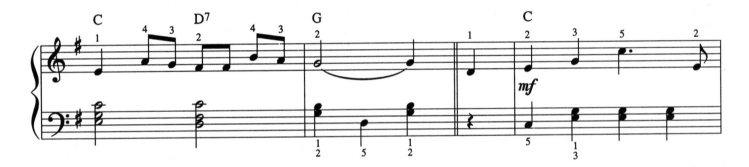

8

Alouette

TRADITIONAL FRENCH-CANADIAN

Moderately fast

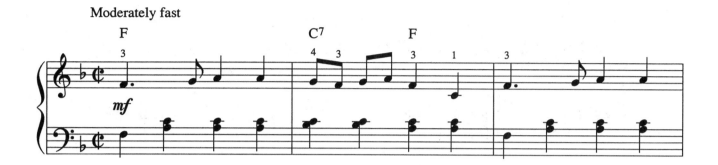

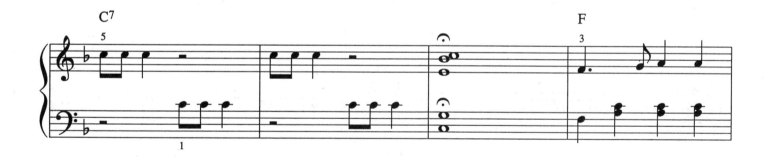

Amazing Grace

TRADITIONAL

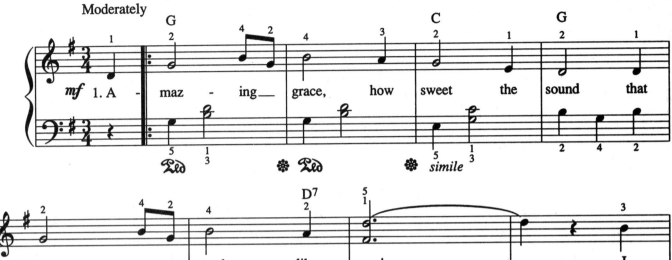

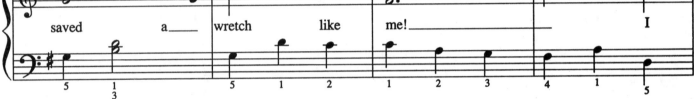

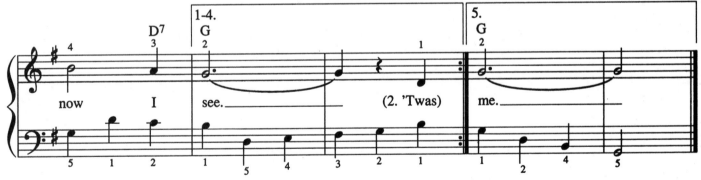

2. 'Twas grace that taught my heart to fear,
   And grace my fears relieved;
   How precious did that grace appear
   The hour I first believed.

3. Thro' many dangers, toils and snares,
   I have already come;
   'Tis grace hath bro't me safe thus far,
   And grace will lead me home.

4. How sweet the name of Jesus sounds
   In a believer's ear.
   It soothes his sorrows, heals his wounds,
   And drives away his fear.

5. Must Jesus bear the cross alone
   And all the world go free?
   No, there's a cross for ev'ry one
   And there's a cross for me.

America
(My Country 'Tis of Thee)

Words by SAMUEL FRANCIS SMITH
Music by H. HARRIS

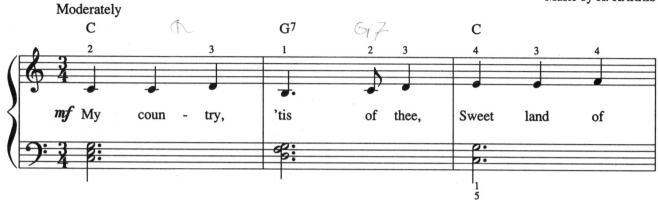

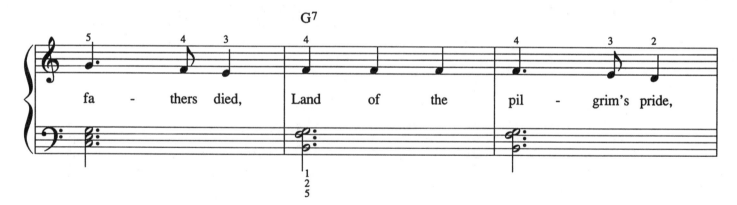

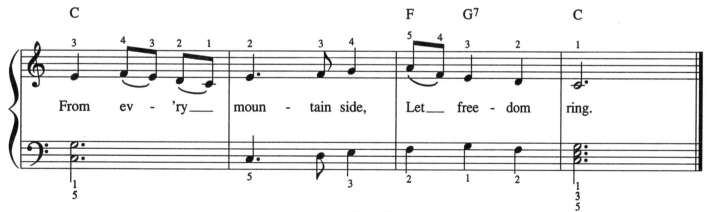

11

Animal Fair

Traditional

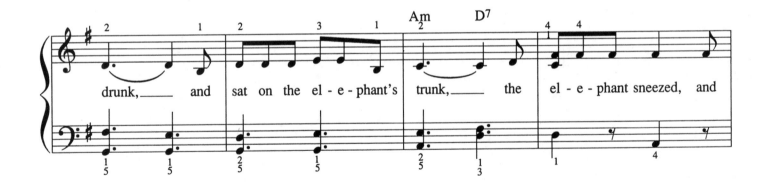

Au Clair de la Lune

Words by Jean Lully
Traditional French Folksong

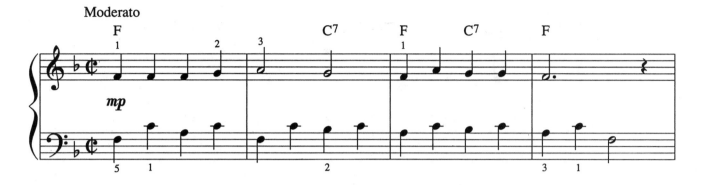

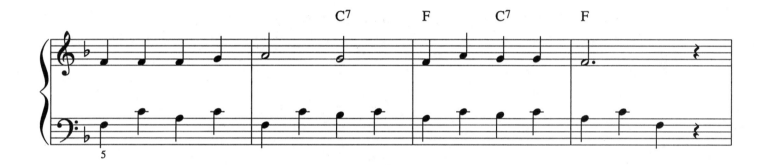

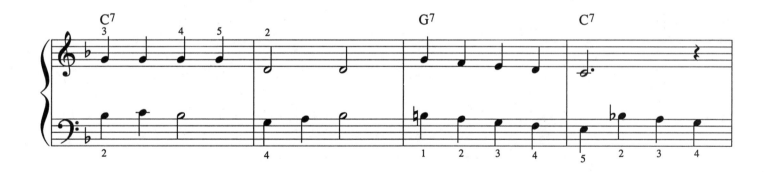

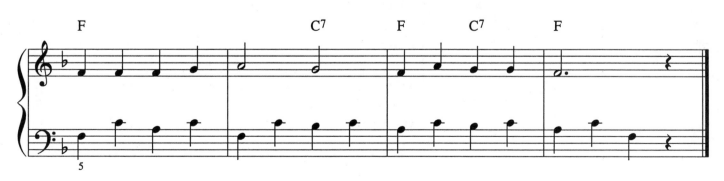

Auld Lang Syne

Words adapted by ROBERT BURNS
TRADITIONAL SCOTTISH FOLKSONG

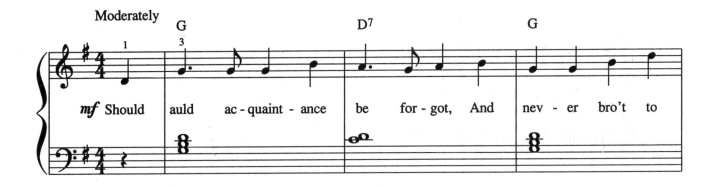

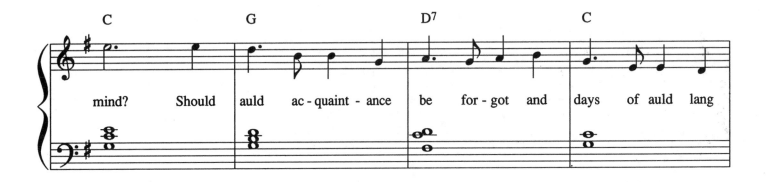

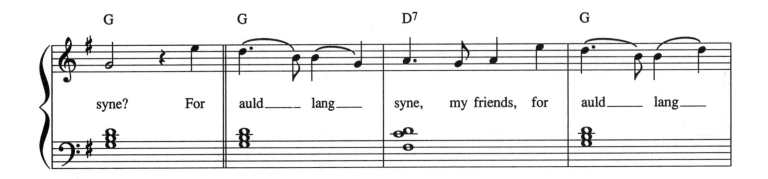

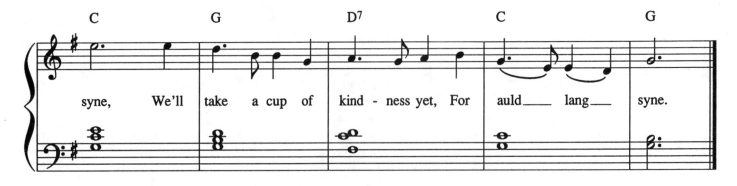

14

Away In A Manger

Words ANONYMOUS
Music by JAMES RAMSEY MURRAY

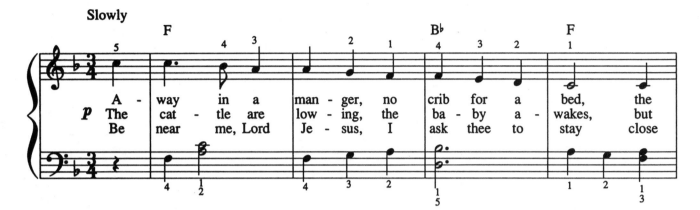

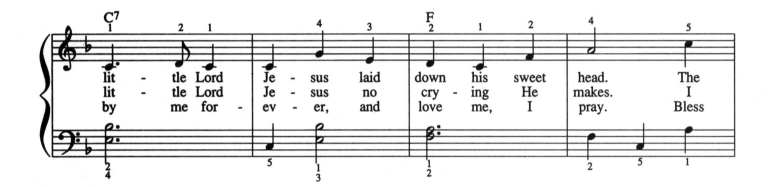

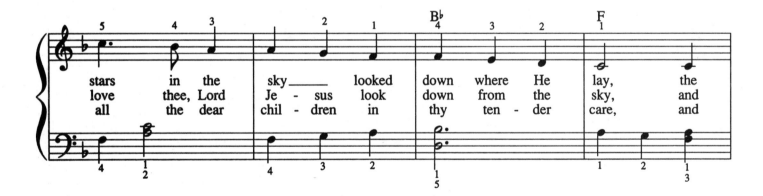

Baa! Baa! Black Sheep

TRADITIONAL FRENCH

The Banana Boat Song

TRADITIONAL

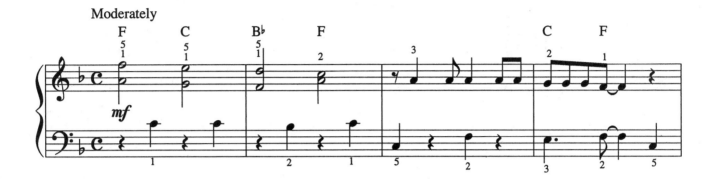

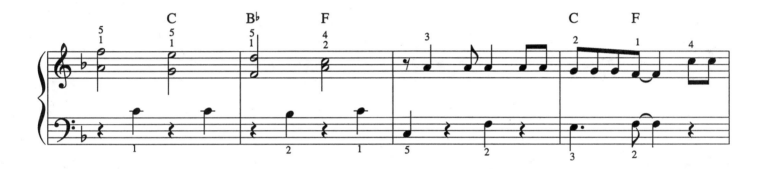

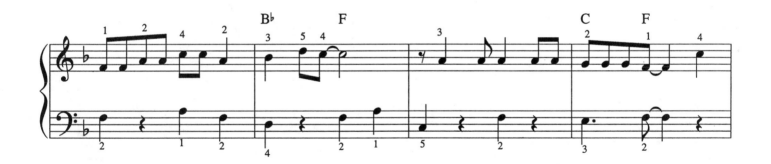

The Battle Cry Of Freedom

Words and Music by
GEORGE FREDERICK ROOT

Believe Me If All Those Endearing Young Charms

Words by THOMAS MOORE
Music by MATTHEW LOCKE

19

Battle Hymn of the Republic

Words by JULIA WARD HOWE
Music by WILLIAM STEFFE

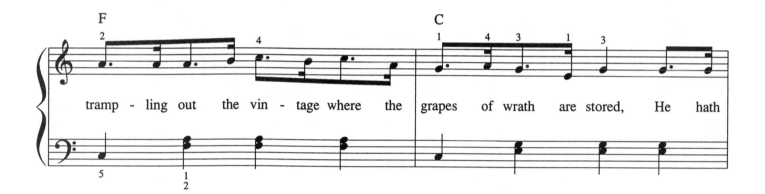

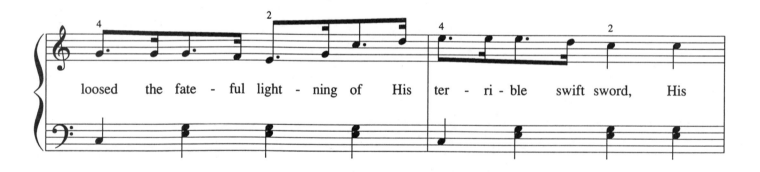

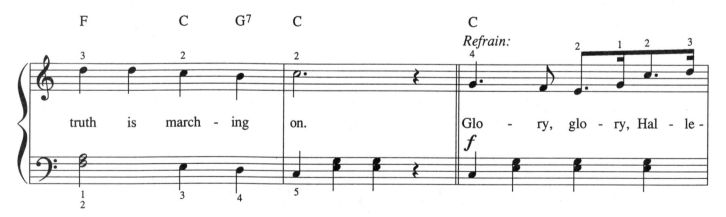

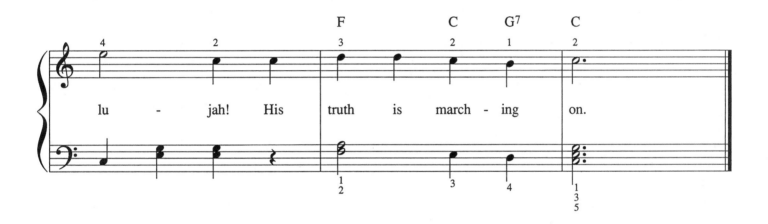

2. I Have seen Him in the watch-fires of a hundred circling camps,
They have builded Him an altar in the evening dews and damps,
I have read His righteous sentence by the dim and flaring lamps,
His day is marching on.

Refrain:

Glory, glory, Hallelujah!
Glory, glory, Hallelujah!
Glory, glory, Hallelujah! . . . His truth is marching on.

The Big Rock Candy Mountain

TRADITIONAL

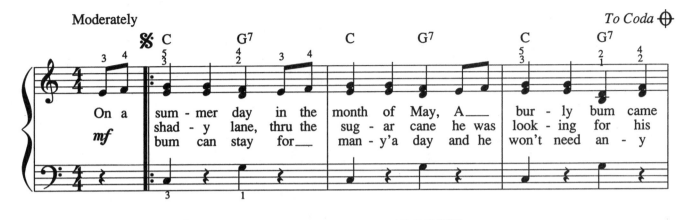

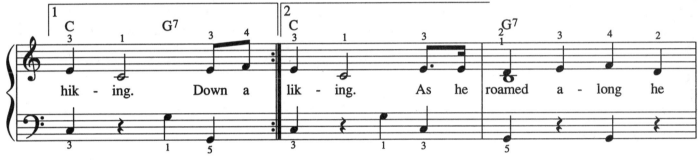

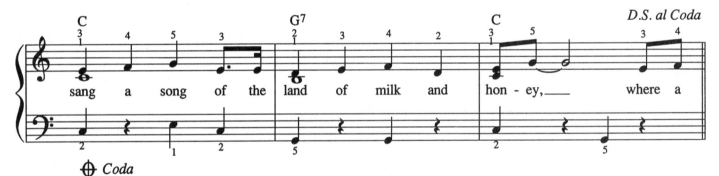

Billy Boy

TRADITIONAL ENGLISH

3. Did she set for you a chair, Billy Boy, Billy Boy,
   Did she set for you a chair, charming Billy?
   Yes, she set for me a chair,
   And the bottom wasn't there,
   She's a young thing and cannot leave her mother.

4. Can she bake a cherry pie, Billy Boy, Billy Boy,
   Can she bake a cherry pie, charming Billy?
   She can bake a cherry pie,
   Quick as a cat can wink her eye,
   She's a young thing and cannot leave her mother.

5. How old is she, Billy Boy, Billy Boy,
   How old is she, charming Billy?
   She's three times six and four times seven.
   Twenty-eight and eleven,
   She's a young thing and cannot leave her mother.

6. Can she sing a pretty song, Billy Boy, Billy Boy,
   Can she sing a pretty song, charming Billy?
   She can sing a pretty song,
   But she gets the words all wrong,
   She's a mother and cannot leave her young thing.

7. Are her eyes very bright, Billy Boy, Billy Boy,
   Are her eyes very bright, charming Billy?
   Yes, her eyes are very bright
   But unfortunately lack sight
   And she can't describe me to her mother.

23

Bill Bailey,
Won't You Please Come Home?

Words and Music by
HUGHIE CANNON

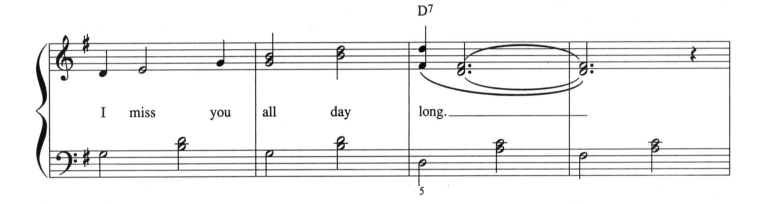

'Mem - ber the rain - y eve - ning I turned you out, With

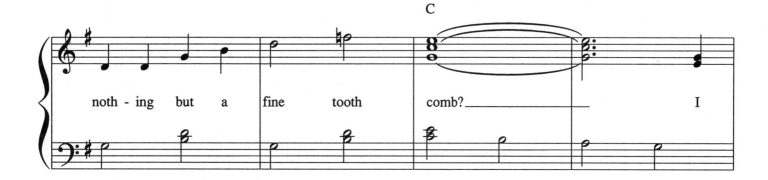

C

noth - ing but a fine tooth comb?_____ I

G

know I'm to blame, Well ain't that a shame? Bill

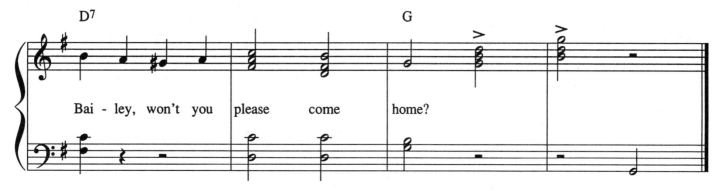

D7   G

Bai - ley, won't you please come home?

Black Is The Color

TRADITIONAL

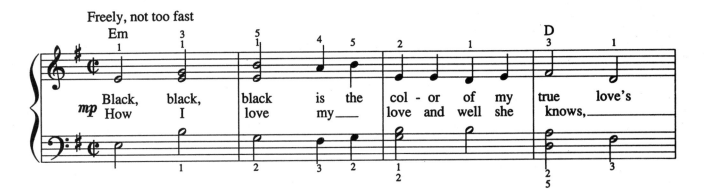

Freely, not too fast

Black, black, black is the col-or of my true love's
How I black love my love and well she knows,

hair. Those lips are like some ros-y fair; the
I love the grass where-on she goes: when

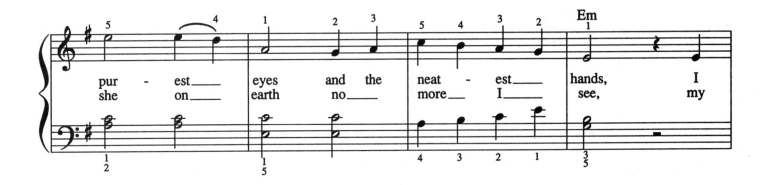

pur - est eyes and the neat - est hands, I
she on earth and no more I see, my

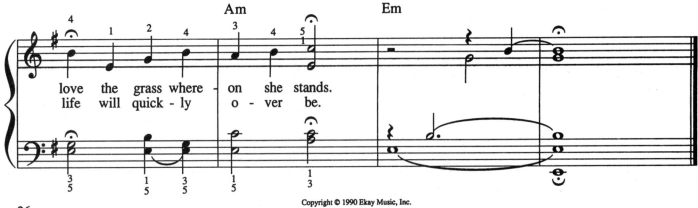

love the grass where - on she stands.
life will quick - ly o - ver be.

Blest Be The Tie That Binds

Words and Music by
JOHN FAWCETT, HANS G. NAEGELI
and KURT KAISER

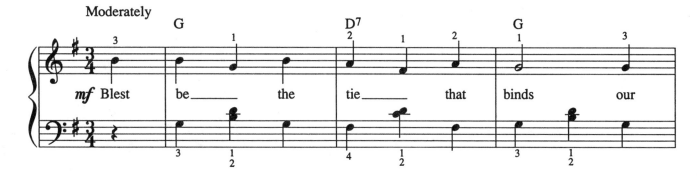

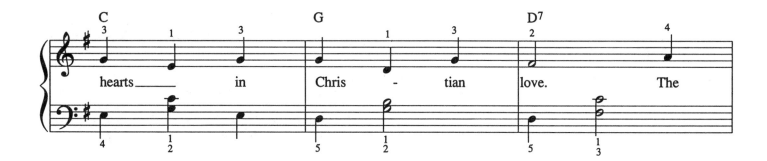

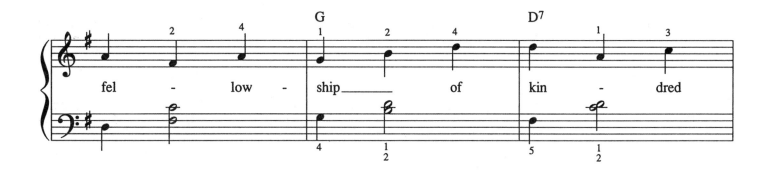

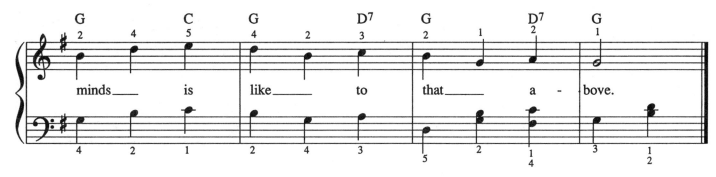

Blue Danube Waltz

By Johann Strauss

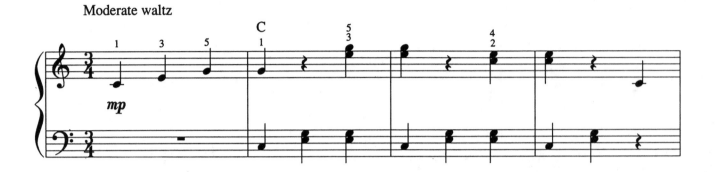

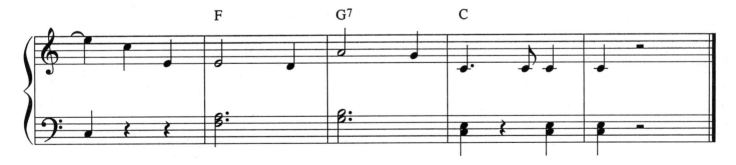

The Bluetail Fly

Words and Music by
DANIEL DECATUR EMMETT

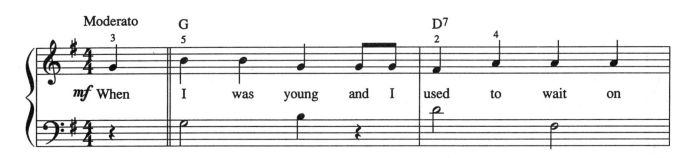

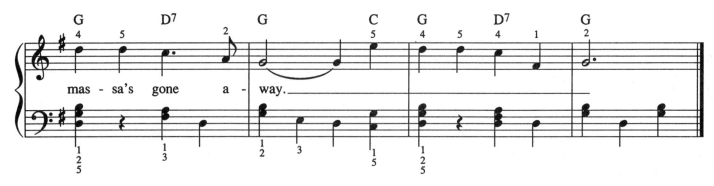

The Boar's Head Carol

TRADITIONAL

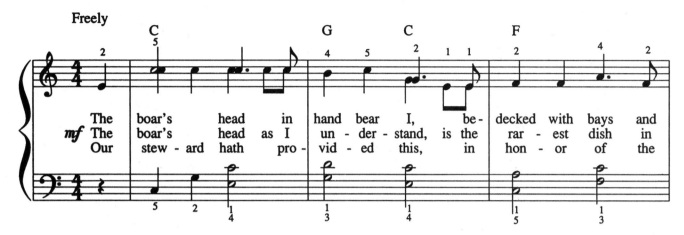

Freely

The boar's head in hand bear I, be-
The boar's head as I un-der-stand, is the
Our stew-ard hath pro-vid-ed this, in

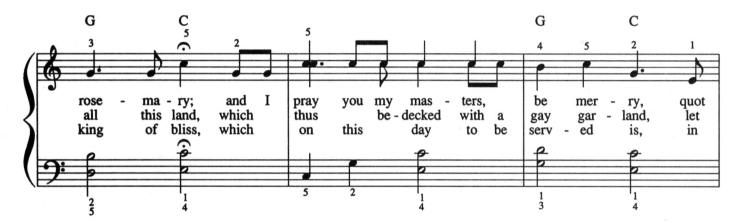

decked with bays and
rar-est dish in
hon-or of in the

rose-ma-ry; and I
all this land, which
king of bliss, which

pray you my mas-ters,
thus be-decked with a
on this day to be

be mer-ry, quot
gay gar-land, let
serv-ed is, in

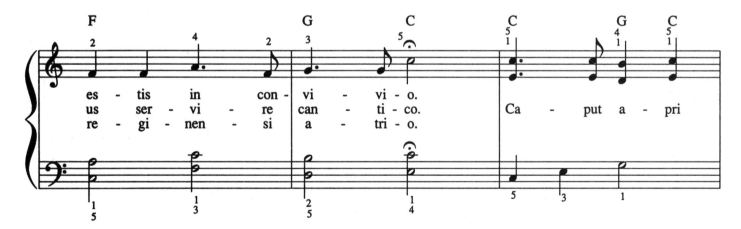

es-tis in con-vi-vi-o.
us ser-vi-re can-ti-co.
re-gi-nen-si a-tri-o.

Ca - put a - pri

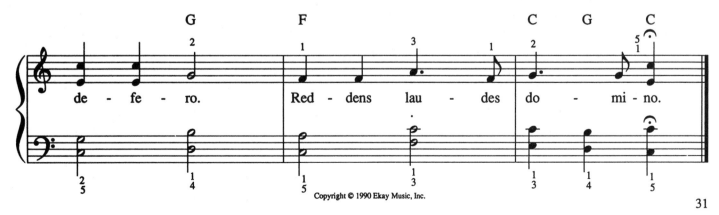

de - fe - ro. Red - dens lau - des do - mi - no.

Bridal Chorus
(from "Lohengrin")

By RICHARD WAGNER

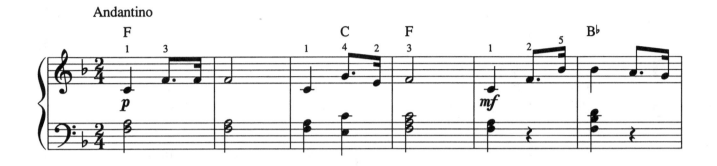

Buffalo Gals

Words and Music by
JOHN HODGES

2. I asked her if she'd stop and talk, stop and talk, stop and talk,
   Her feet took up the whole sidewalk, and left no room for me.

3. I asked her if she'd be my wife, be my wife, be my wife,
   Then I'd be happy all my life, if she'd marry me.

Bury Me Not
On The Lone Prairie

Words by E.H. CHAPIN
Music by GEORGE N. ALLEN

3. "I've always wished to be laid when I died
In the little churchyard on the green hillside;
By my father's grave there let mine be,
And Bury Me Not On The Lone Prairie."

4. "Oh, bury me not" – and his voice failed there,
But we took no heed of his dying prayer.
In a narrow grave, just six by three,
We buried him on the lone prairie.

5. And the cowboys now, as they roam the plain,
(For they marked the spot where his bones were lain)
Fling a handful of roses over the grave,
With a Prayer to Him who his soul will save.

6. "Oh, Bury Me Not On The Lone Prairie,
Where the wolves can howl and growl o'er me.
Fling a handful of roses over my grave,
With a prayer to Him who my soul will save."

The Campbells Are Coming

TRADITIONAL SCOTTISH

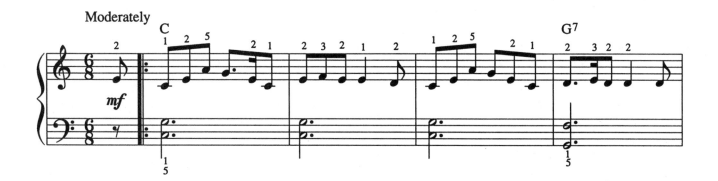

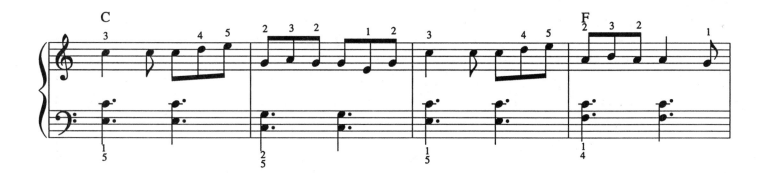

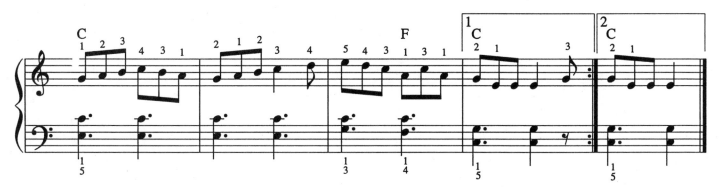

The Camptown Races

Words and Music by
STEPHEN FOSTER

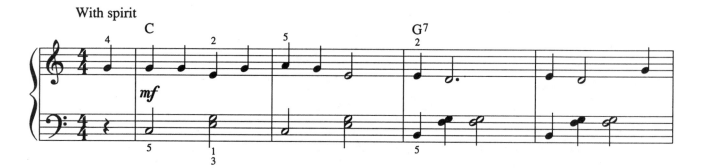

Careless Love

TRADITIONAL

Rather slowly (with expression)

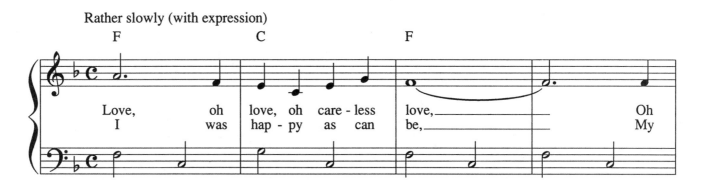

Love, oh love, oh care - less love,_____ Oh My
I was hap - py as can be,_____

love, oh love, oh care - less love._____ My
days were sun - ny, bright and free._____ You

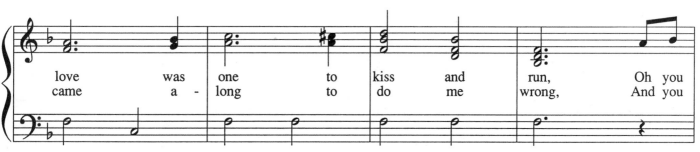

love was one to kiss and run, Oh you
came a - long to do me wrong, And you

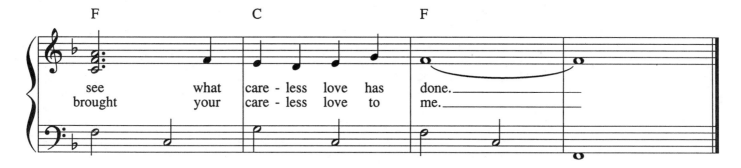

see what care - less love has done._____
brought your care - less love to me._____

Carry Me Back to Old Virginny

Words and Music by
JAMES A. BLAND

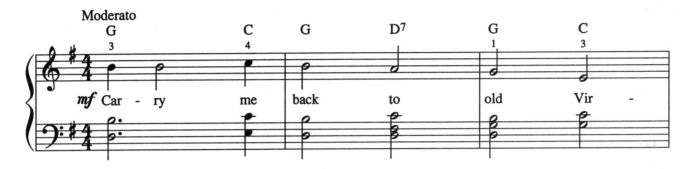

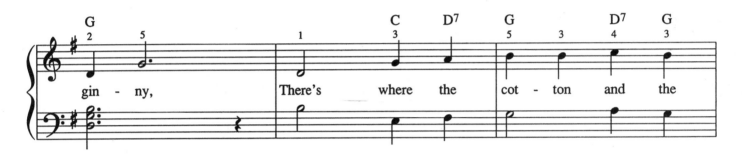

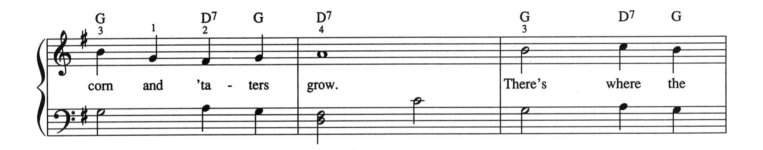

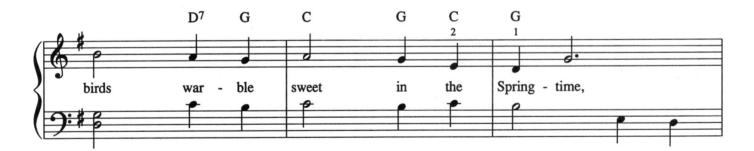

38

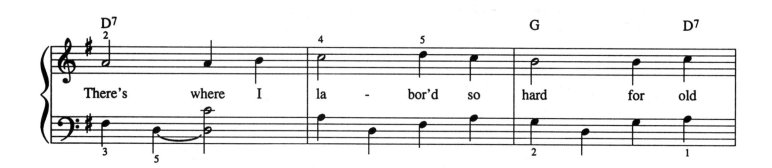

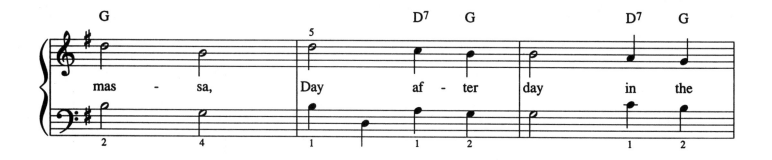

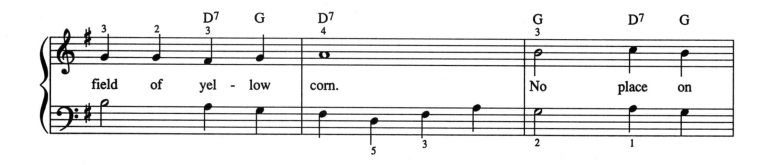

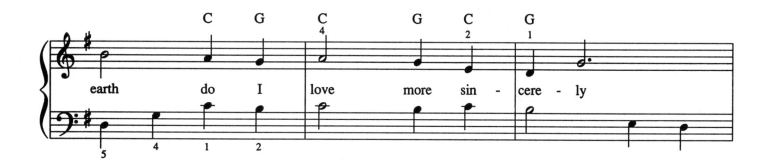

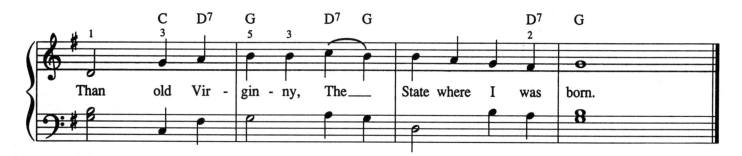

Chiapanecas

TRADITIONAL MEXICAN

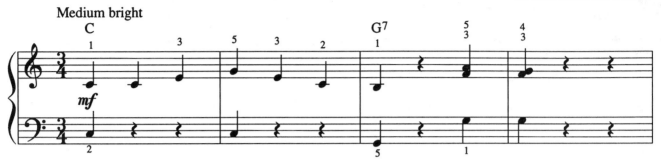

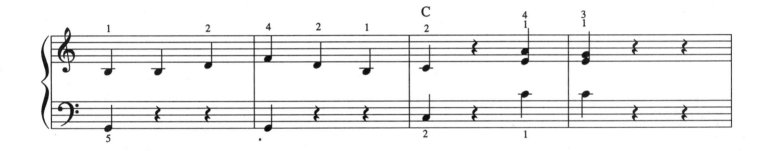

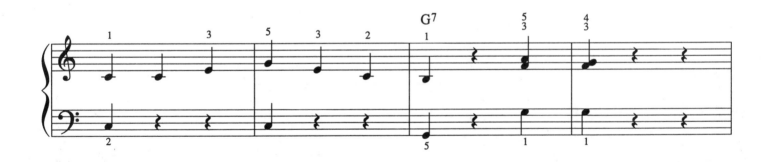

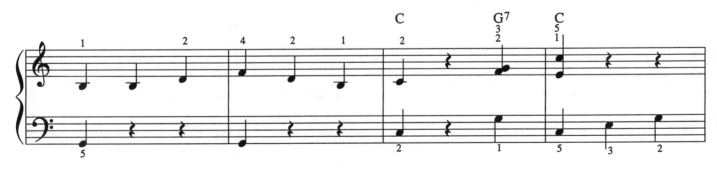

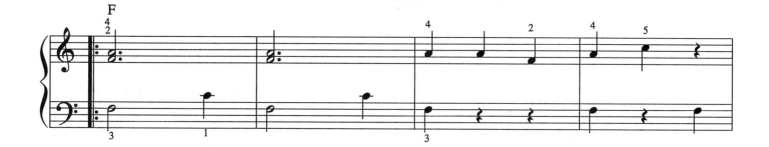

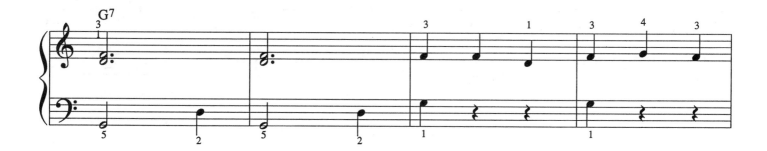

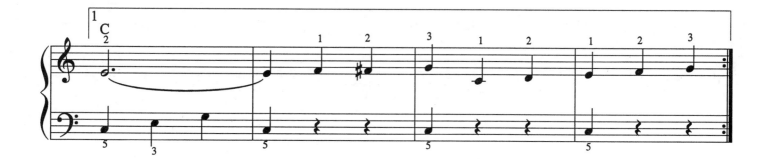

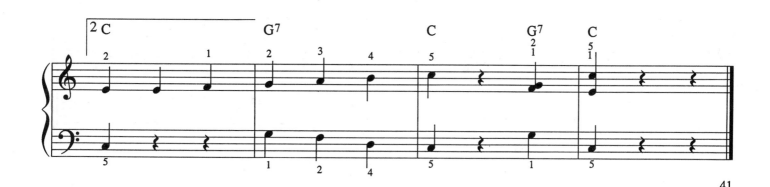

41

Chopsticks

By Arthur De Lulli

Lightly - medium bright

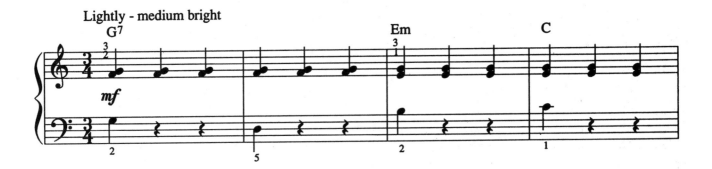

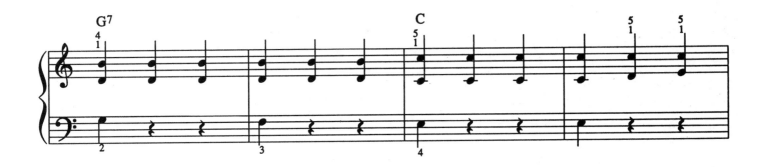

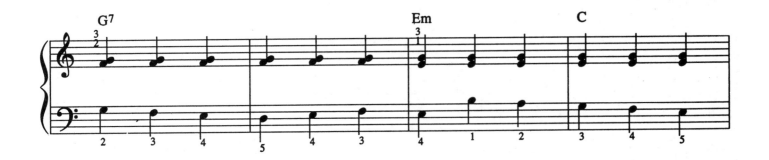

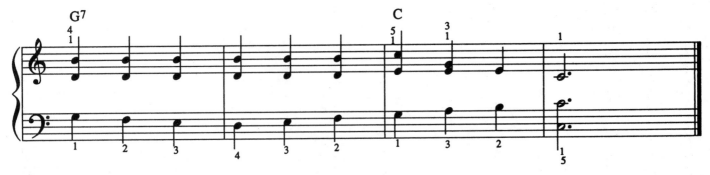

The Church In The Wildwood

Words and Music by
WILLIAM S. PITTS

3. From the church in the valley by the wildwood,
When day fades away into night;
I would fain from this spot of my childhood
Wing my way to the mansions of light.

Come, Josephine, In My Flying Machine

Words by ALFRED BRYAN
Music by FRED FISHER

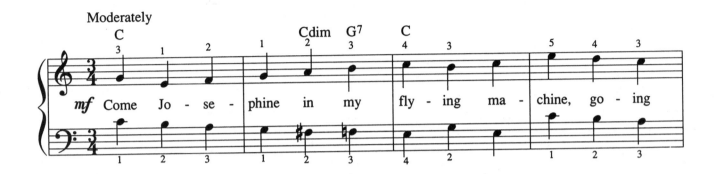

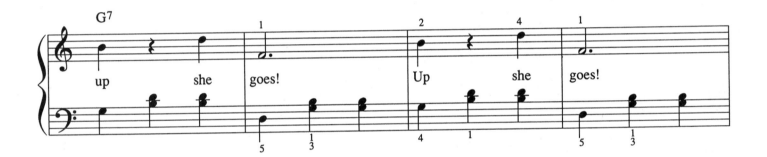

Up, up, a lit - tle bit

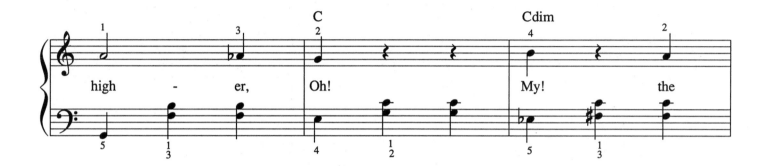

high - er, Oh! My! the

moon is on fire._____ Come Jo - se -

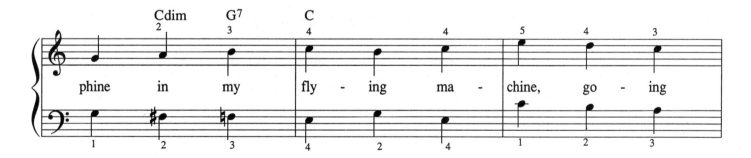

phine in my fly - ing ma - chine, go - ing

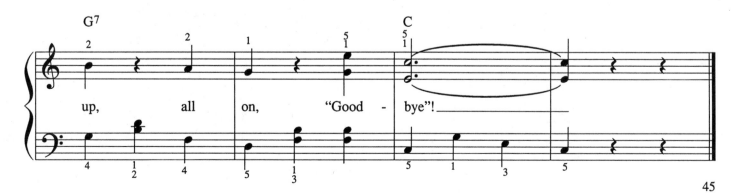

up, all on, "Good - bye"!_____

Comin' Thro' the Rye

Words by ROBERT BURNS
Music TRADITIONAL SCOTTISH

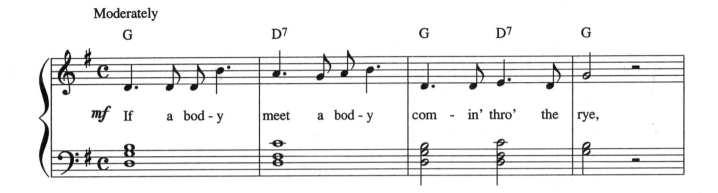

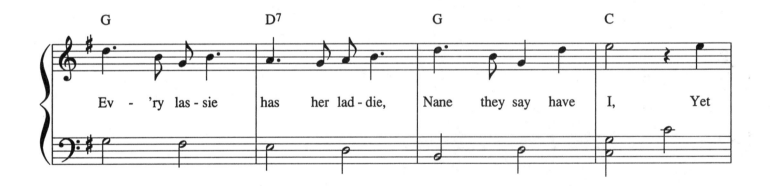

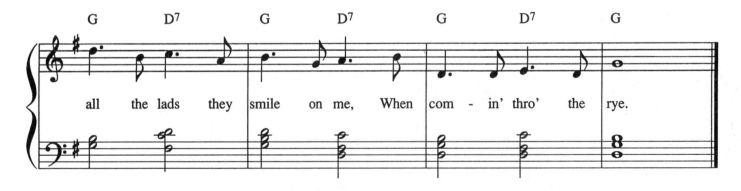

Country Gardens

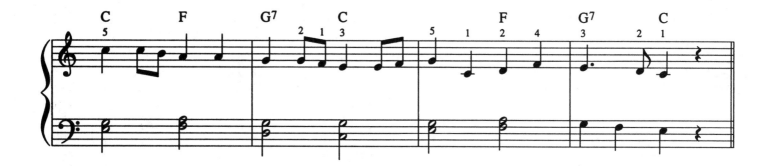

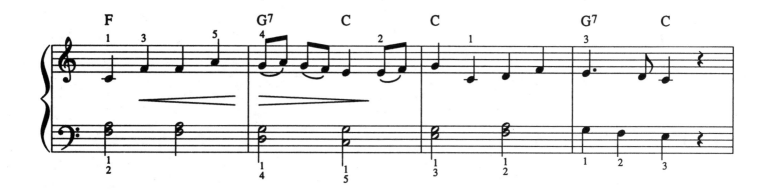

Cradle Song

By JOHANNES BRAHMS

Dark Eyes

TRADITIONAL RUSSIAN

Valse moderato

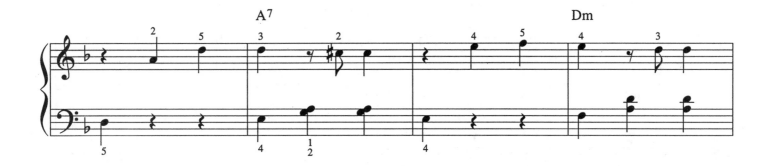

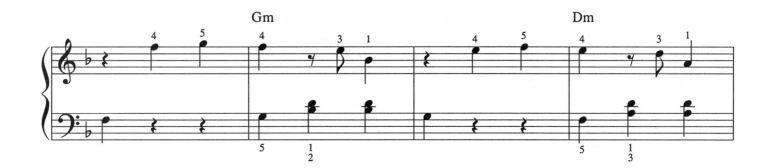

Daisy Bell
(A Bicycle Built For Two)

Words and Music by
HARRY DACRE

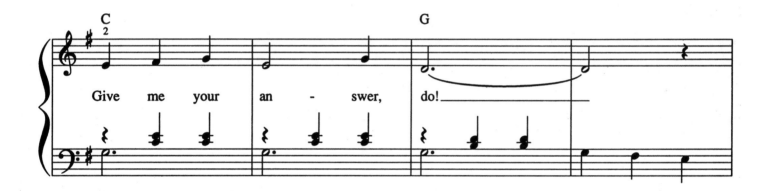

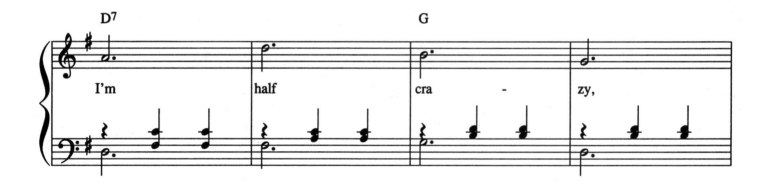

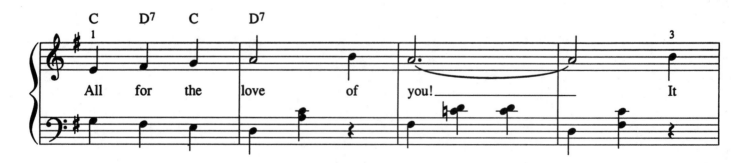

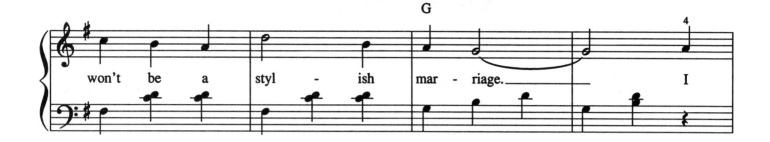

won't be a styl - ish mar - riage.___ I

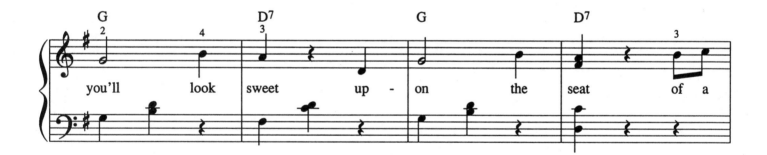

can't af - ford a car - riage,___ But

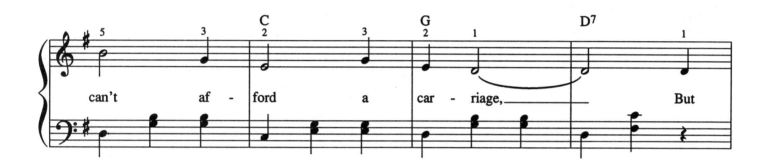

you'll look sweet up - on the seat of a

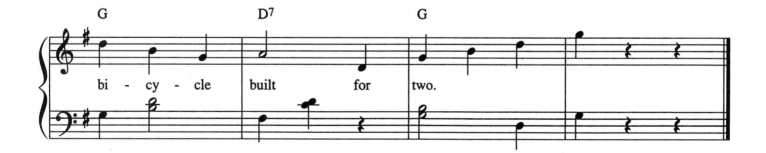

bi - cy - cle built for two.

Deck the Hall

Words ANONYMOUS
Music TRADITIONAL WALES

Brightly

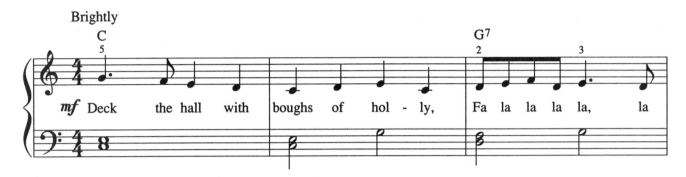

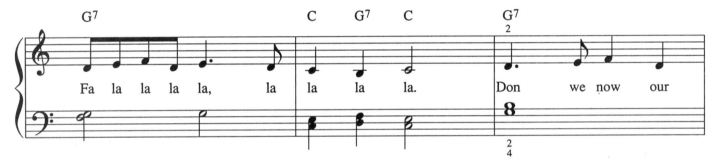

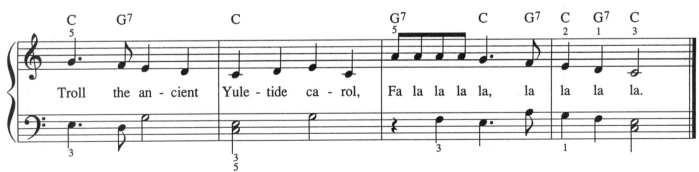

Did You Ever See A Lassie?

ANONYMOUS

Did you e - ver see a las - sie, a las - sie, a las - sie, did you

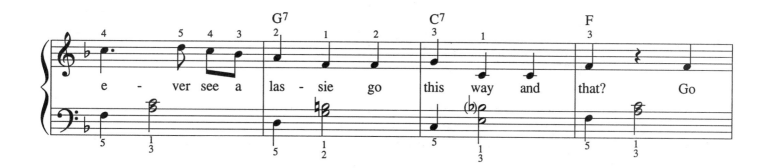

e - ver see a las - sie go this way and that? Go

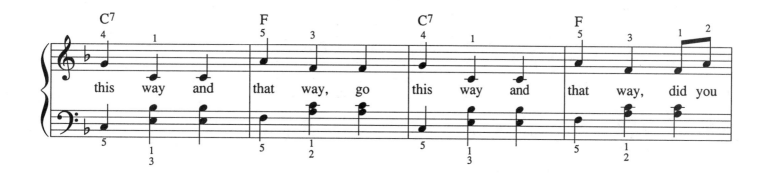

this way and that way, go this way and that way, did you

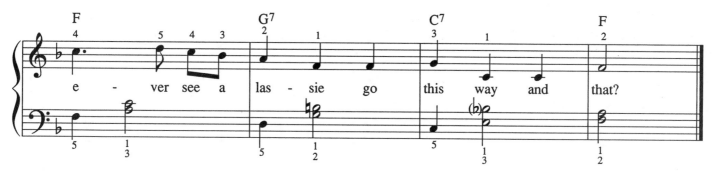

e - ver see a las - sie go this way and that?

Dixie

Words and Music by
DAN EMMETT

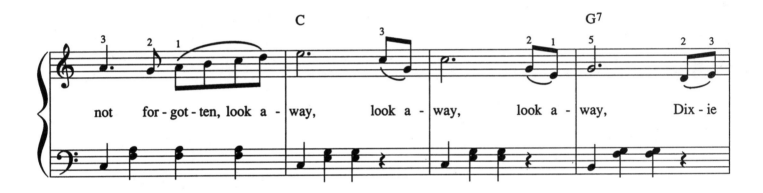

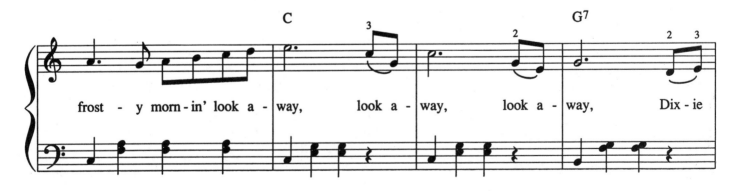

54

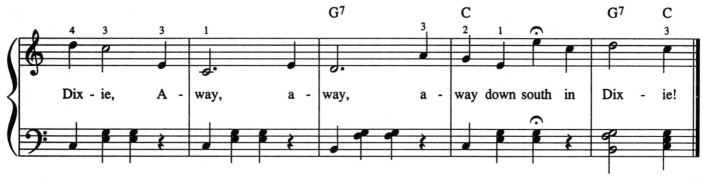

Down by the Riverside

TRADITIONAL

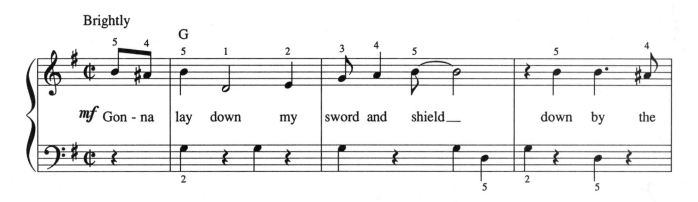

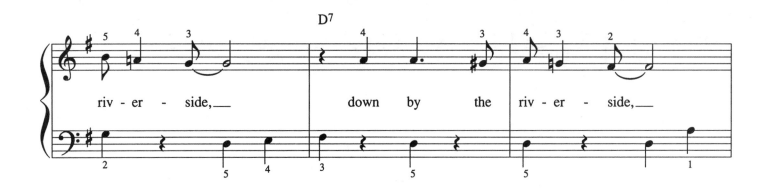

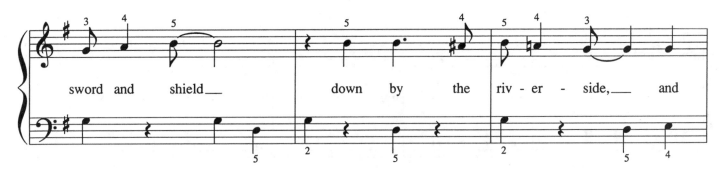

56

Chorus:

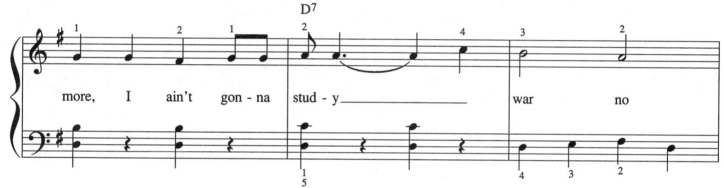

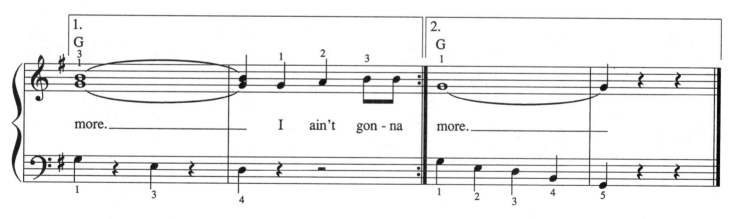

2. I'm gonna join hands with everyone,
   Down By The Riverside, Down By The Riverside,
   Down By The Riverside,
   I'm gonna join hands with everyone,
   Down By The Riverside,
   And study war no more.

3. I'm gonna put on my long white robe . . .

4. I'm gonna walk with the Prince of Peace . . .

Down By The Station

TRADITIONAL

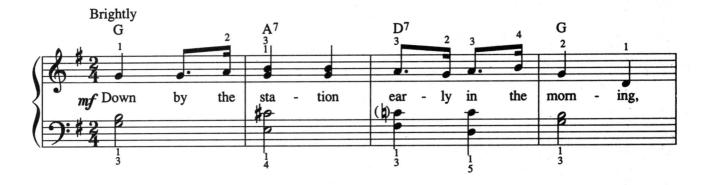

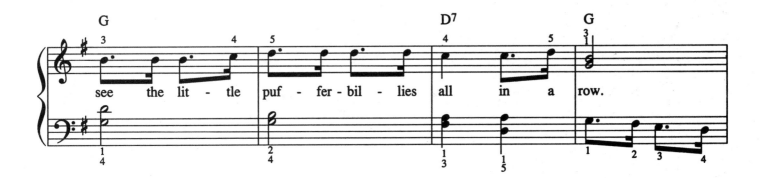

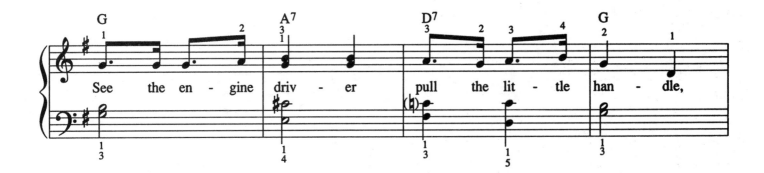

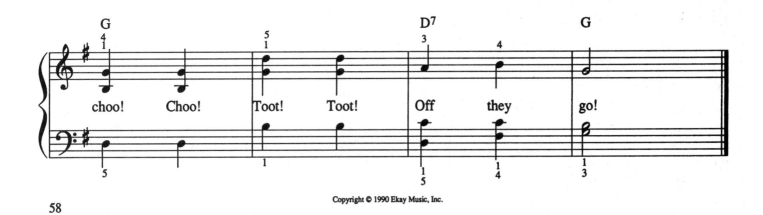

Down in the Valley

TRADITIONAL

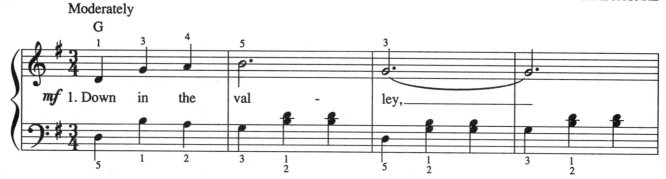

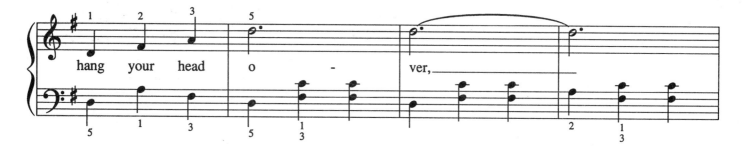

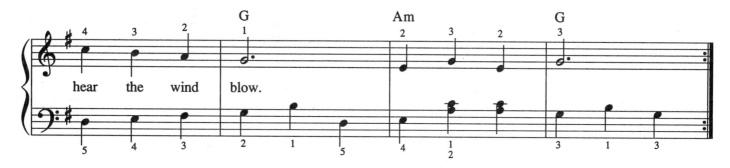

2. Roses love sunshine, violets love dew
   Angels in heaven, know I love you.
   Know I love dear, know I love you.
   Angels in heaven, know I love you.

3. If you don't love me, love whom you please
   Throw your arms round me, give my heart ease.
   Give my heart ease love, give my heart ease.
   Throw your arms round me, give my heart ease.

4. Build me a castle forty feet high
   So I can see him as he rides by
   As he rides by love, as he rides by
   So I can see him as he rides by.

5. Write me a letter, send it by mail
   Send it in care of Birmingham jail.
   Birmingham jail love, Birmingham jail
   Send it in care of Birmingham jail.

59

Drink to Me
Only with Thine Eyes

Words by BEN JONSON
Music by COLONEL R. MELLISH

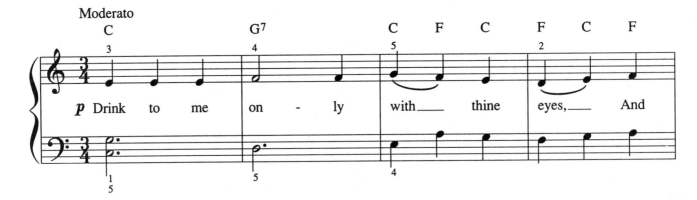

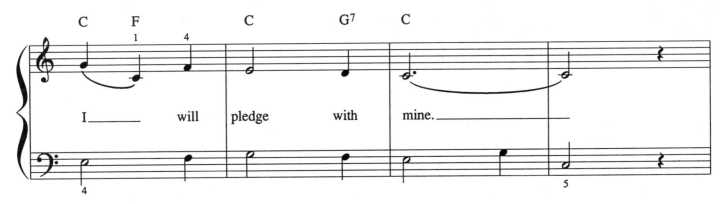

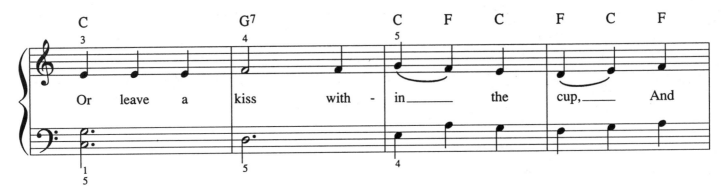

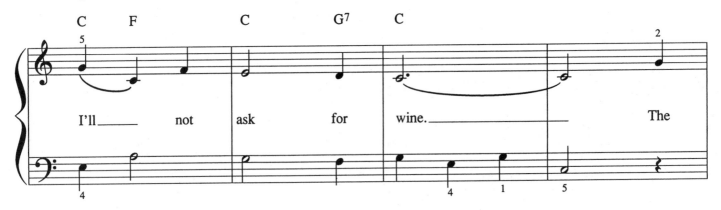

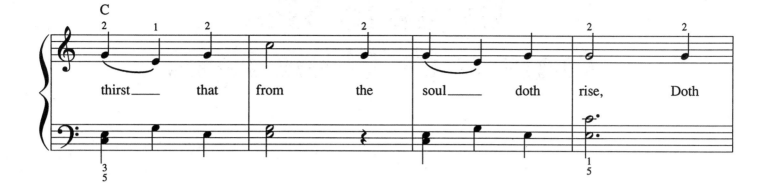

thirst____ that from the soul____ doth rise, Doth

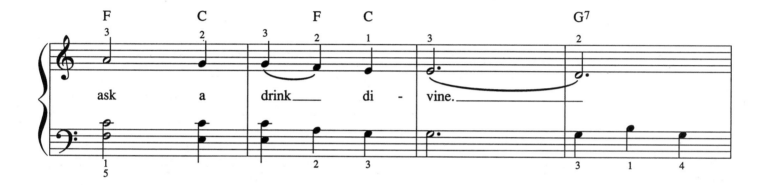

ask a drink____ di - vine.____

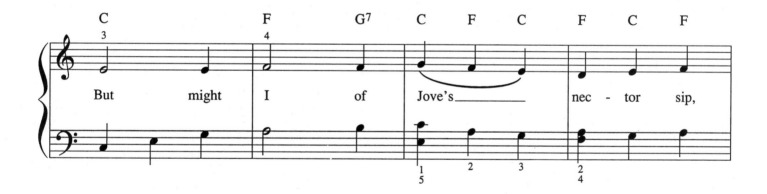

But might I of Jove's____ nec - tor sip,

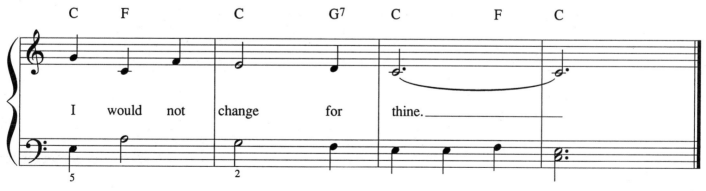

I would not change for thine.____

The Drunken Sailor

TRADITIONAL

3. Pull out the plug and wet him all over,
Pull out the plug and wet him all over,
Pull out the plug and wet him all over,
Early in the morning.
Chorus

4. Tie him to the top mast when she's under,
Tie him to the top mast when she's under,
Tie him to the top mast when she's under,
Early in the morning.
Chorus

5. Put him in the scuppers with the hosepipe on him,
Put him in the scuppers with the hosepipe on him,
Put him in the scuppers with the hosepipe on him,
Early in the morning.
Chorus

Eency, Weency Spider

TRADITIONAL

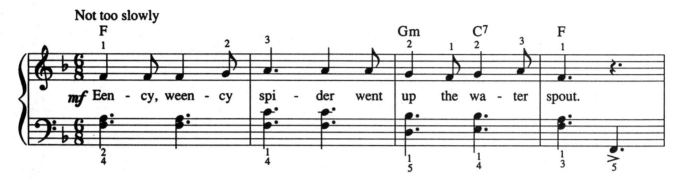

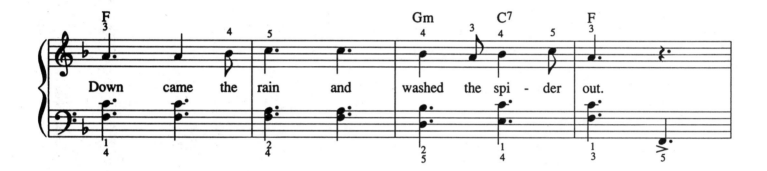

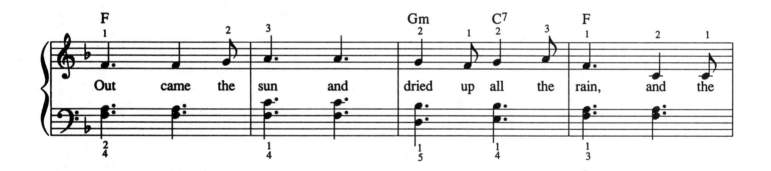

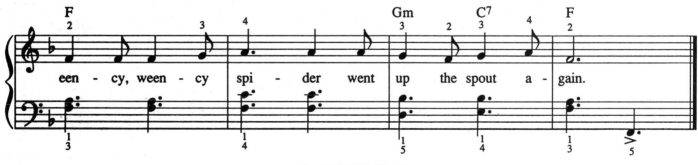

Ev'ry Time I Feel the Spirit

TRADITIONAL

Moderately (with a steady beat)

The Foggy, Foggy Dew

TRADITIONAL ENGLISH

2. One night she came to my bedside,
When I was fast asleep,
She flung her arms around my neck
And then began to weep.
She wept, she cried, she tore her hair,
Ah me, what could I do?
So all night long I held her in my arms,
Just to keep her from the foggy, foggy dew.

3. Still I am a bachelor, I live with my son,
We work at the weaver's trade.
And every time I look into his eyes
He reminds me of that fair young maid.
He reminds me of the winter time,
And part of the summer, too,
And of the many, many times I held her in my arms,
Just to keep her from the foggy, foggy dew.

65

For He's a Jolly Good Fellow

TRADITIONAL

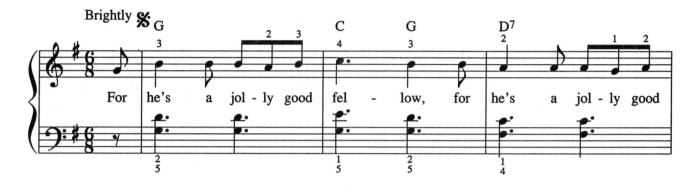

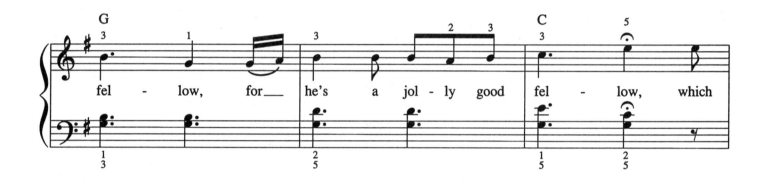

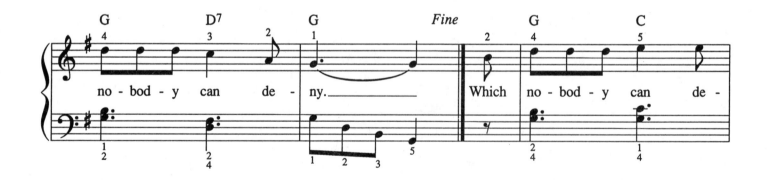

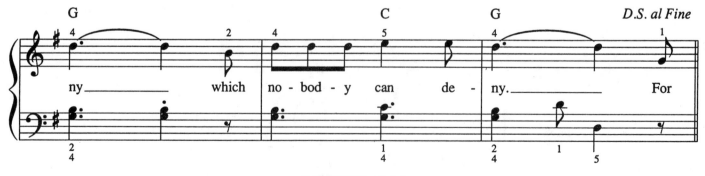

66

Frankie and Johnny

ANONYMOUS

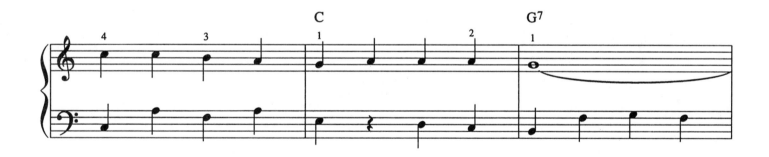

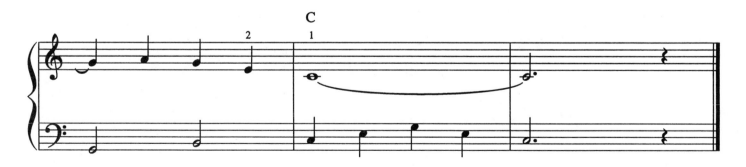

Frère Jacques

TRADITIONAL FRENCH

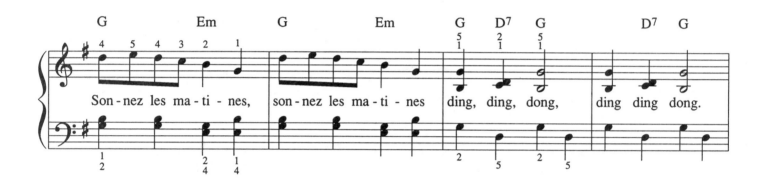

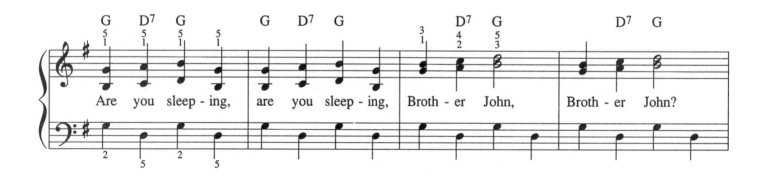

The Glow Worm

By Paul Lincke

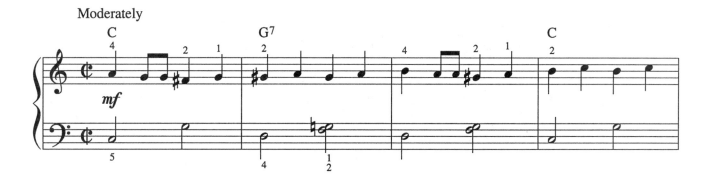

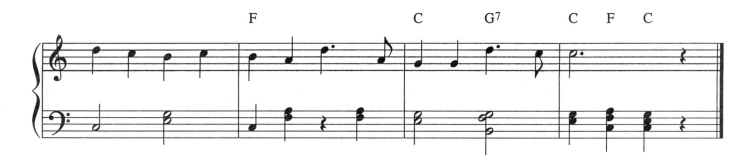

Go Down, Moses

TRADITIONAL

Slowly

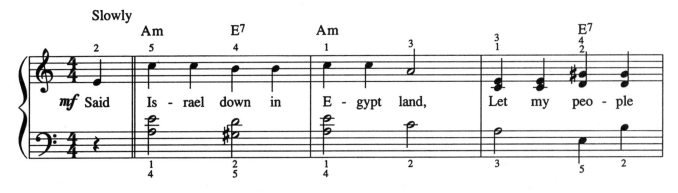

Said Is - rael down in E - gypt land, Let my peo - ple

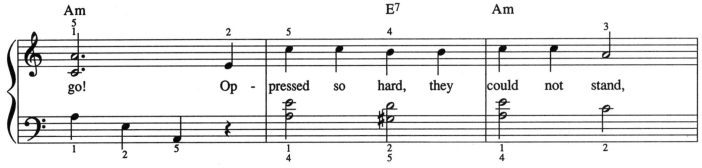

go! Op - pressed so hard, they could not stand,

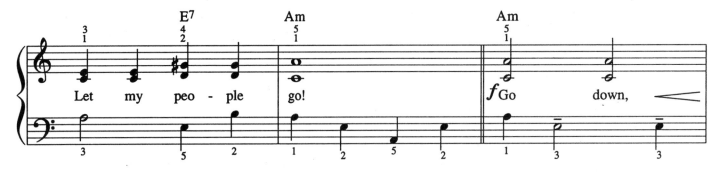

Let my peo - ple go! Go down,

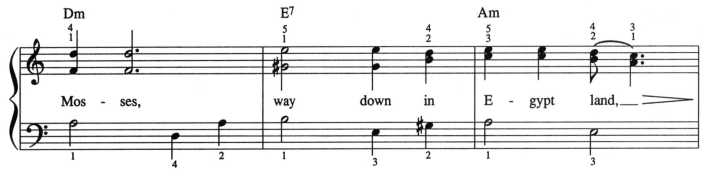

Mos - ses, way down in E - gypt land, Go and tell

Pha - roah to let my peo - ple go!

Go Tell Aunt Rhody

TRADITIONAL

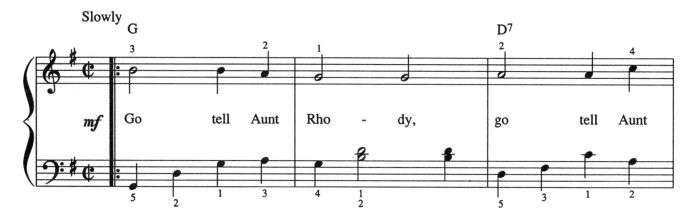

Slowly

Go tell Aunt Rho - dy, go tell Aunt

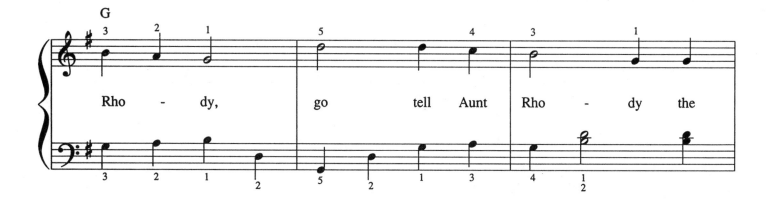

Rho - dy, go tell Aunt Rho - dy the

old grey goose is dead. *2. The* head.

2. The one she was saving, *(three times)*
To make a feather bed.

3. The gander is weeping, *(three times)*
Because his wife is dead.

4. The goslings are crying, *(three times)*
Because their mama's dead.

5. She died in the water, *(three times)*
With her heels above her head.

Good Night, Ladies

Words by E.P. Christy
and F.V.D. Garretson
Music Traditional

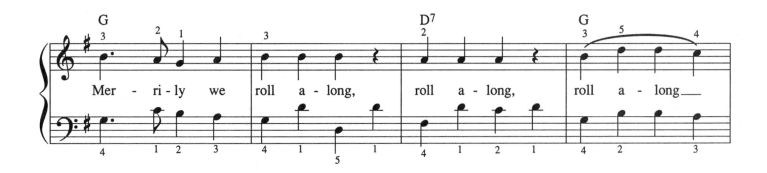

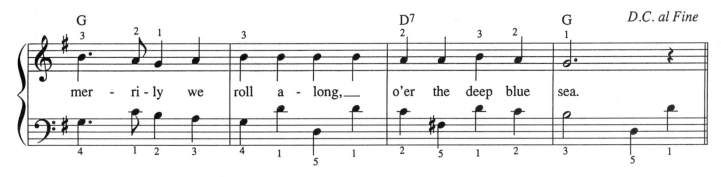

Goodbye, Old Paint

TRADITIONAL

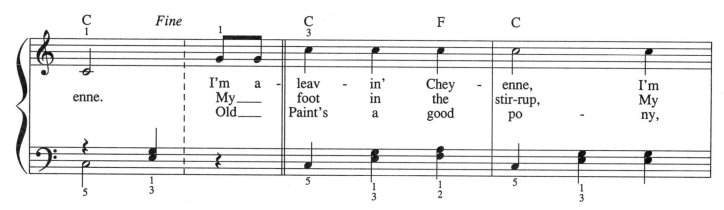

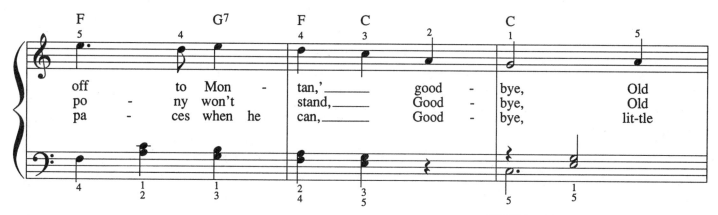

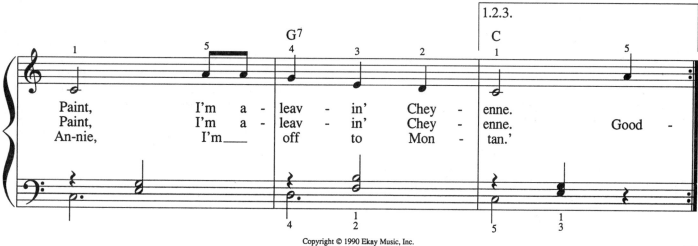

73

Green Grow the Lilacs

ANONYMOUS

Slowly and tenderly

mf Green grow the li - lacs all spark - ling with dew, I'm lone - ly, my dar - ling, since part - ing with you. But by our next meet - ing I hope to prove true, And change the green li - lacs to the red, white and blue.

2. I used to have a sweetheart, but now I have none,
Since she's gone and left me, I care not for one.
Since she's gone and left me, contented I"ll be,
For she loves another one better than me.

3. I passed my love's window, both early and late,
The look that she gave me, it made my heart ache.
Oh, the look that she gave me was painful to see,
For she loves another one better than me.

4. I wrote my love letters in rosy red line,
She sent me an answer all twisted in twines,
Saying, "Keep your love letters and don't waste your time,
Just you write to your love and I'll write to mine."

Hail! Hail!
The Gang's All Here

Words by THEDORA MORSE
Music by THEODORE MORSE

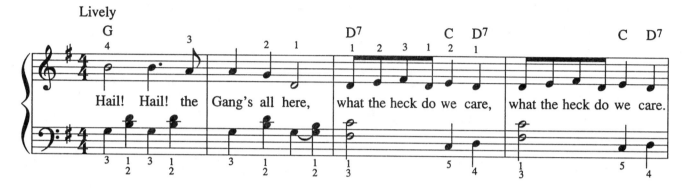

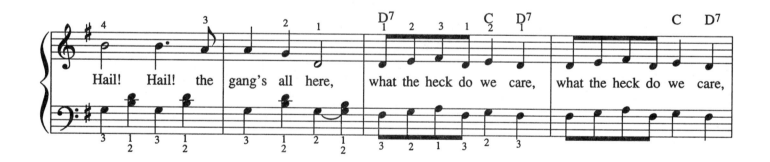

Guantanamera

Words by José Marti
Music Traditional Latin American

Not too slowly

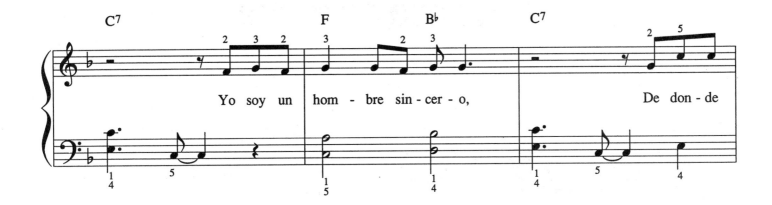

Yo soy un hom - bre sin - cer - o, De don - de

cre - ce la pal - ma,___ Y antes de mor - ir - me quie -

D.S. ℅ al Fine

ro, E - char mis ver - sos del al - ma.

2. *Mi verso es de un verde claro,*
   Y de un carmin encendido,
   Mi verso es de un verde claro,
   Y de un carmin encendido,
   Mi verso es un ciervo herido,
   Que busca en el monte amparo.
   (Chorus)

3. *Con los pobres de la tierra,*
   Quiero yo mi suerte echar,
   Con los pobres de la tierra,
   Quiero yo mi suerte echar,
   El arroyo de la sierra,
   Me complace mas que el mar.
   (Chorus)

Hava Nagilah

TRADITIONAL JEWISH

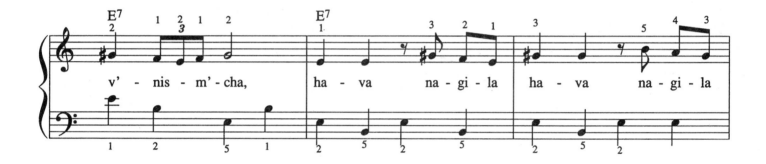

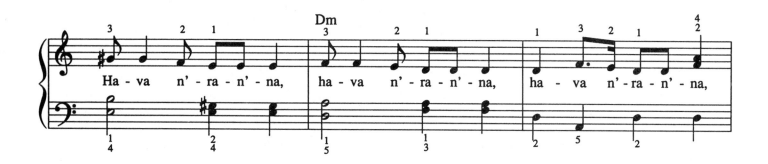

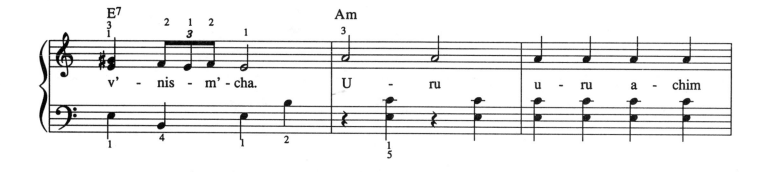

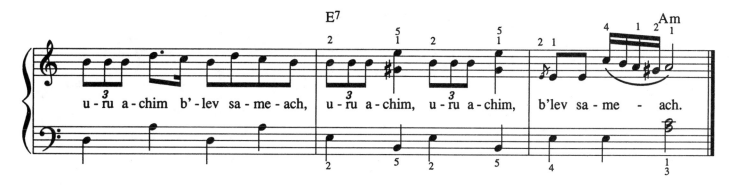

He's Got the Whole World in His Hands

TRADITIONAL

Moderately

Hello! Ma Baby

Words and Music by
IDA EMERSON and JOSEPH E. HOWARD

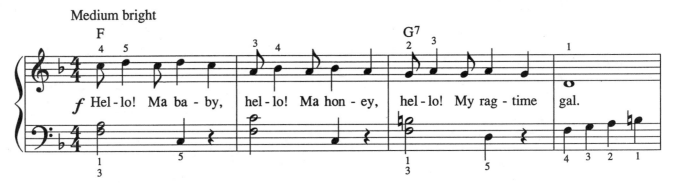

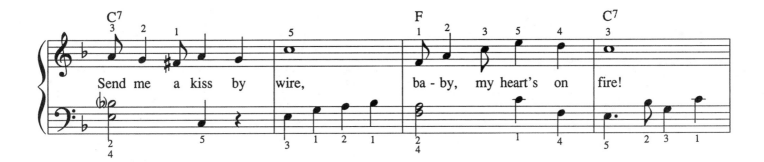

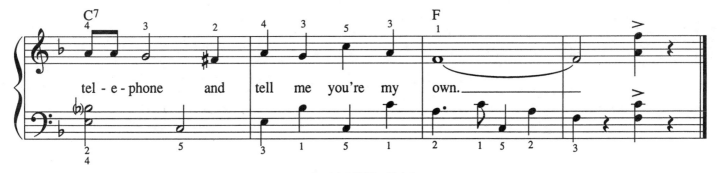

Hey, Ho! Nobody Home

TRADITIONAL

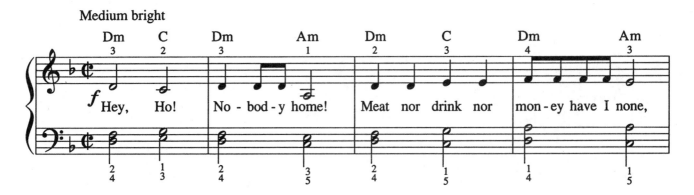

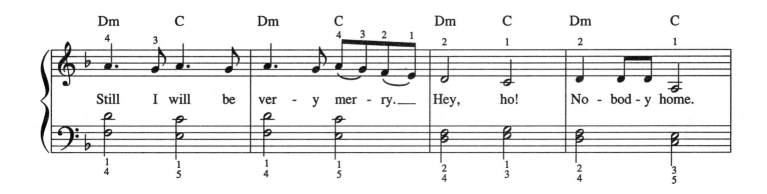

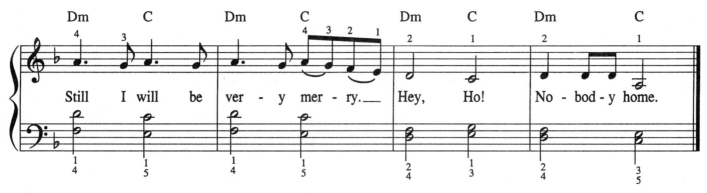

The Holly And The Ivy

TRADITIONAL

4. The holly bears a prickle,
   As sharp as any thorn
   And Mary bore sweet Jesus Christ
   On Christmas Day in the morn.
   (Refrain)

5. The holly bears a bark,
   As bitter as any gall,
   And Mary bore sweet Jesus Christ
   For to redeem us all.
   (Refrain)

Home On The Range

Words by BREWSTER HIGLEY
Music by DANIEL E. KELLEY

Moderately

Home Sweet Home

Words by John Howard Payne
Music adapted by Sir Henry Rowley Bishop

Tenderly

mf Mid___ pleas - ures and pal - ac - es tho'___
ev - er so hum - ble, there's no___

we may roam,___ be it
place like

home.___ A charm

from the sky seems to hal - low us

there,___ which seek thro' the world

is ne'er met___ with else - where.___

85

A Hot Time in the Old Town Tonight

Words by Joe Hayden
Music by Theodore A. Metz

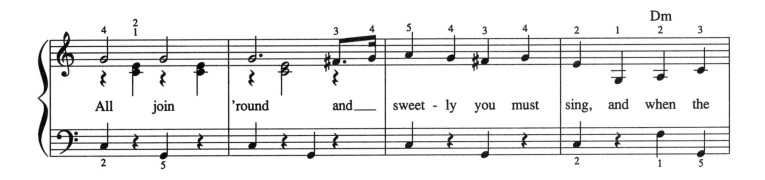

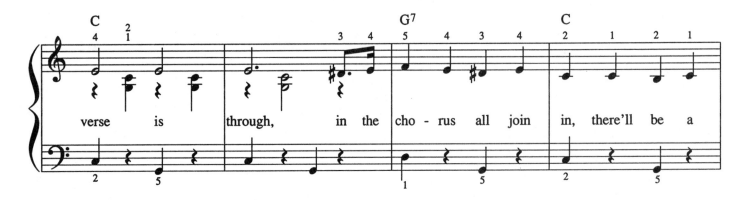

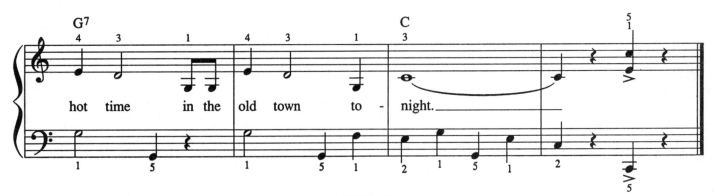

How Dry I Am

TRADITIONAL

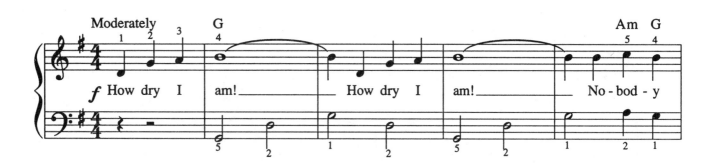

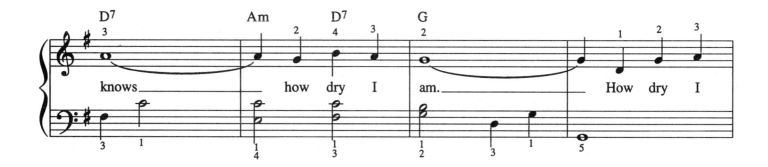

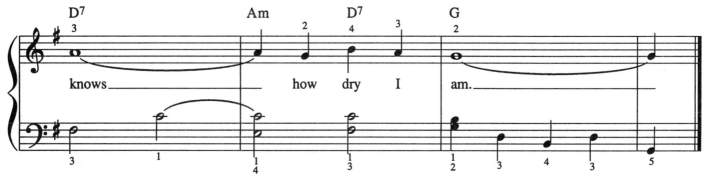

I Love You Truly

Words and Music by
CARRIE JACOBS-BOND

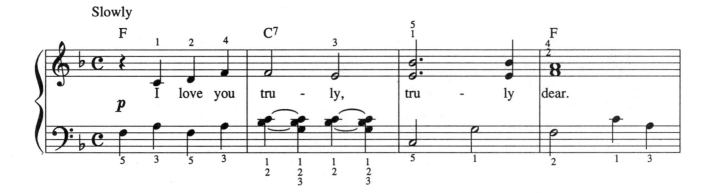

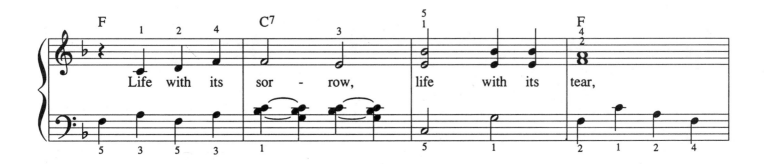

I Saw Three Ships

TRADITIONAL

If You're Happy
(And You Know It)

TRADITIONAL

In the Sweet Bye and Bye

Words by S.F. BENNETT
Music by J.P. WEBSTER

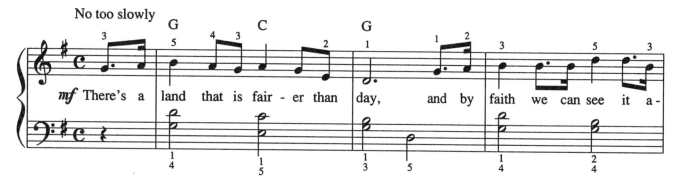

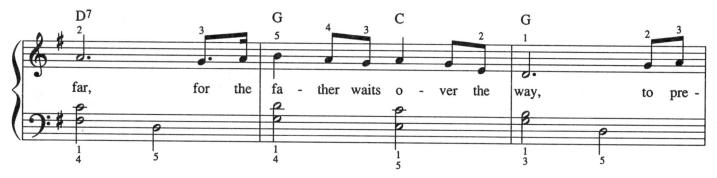

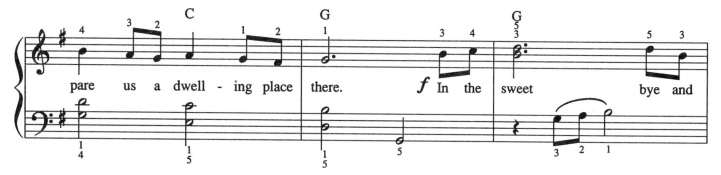

Irish Washerwoman

TRADITIONAL IRISH

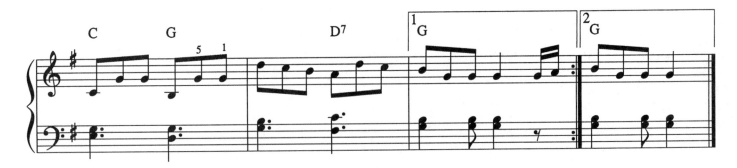

Jingle Bells

Words and Music by
J.S. PIERPONT

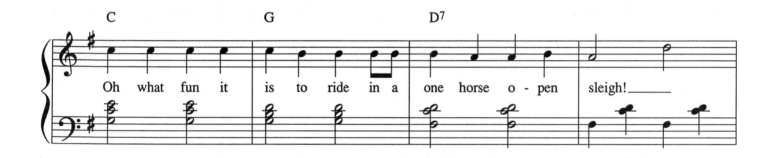

Joshua Fought The Battle Of Jericho

TRADITIONAL

Kum-Bah-Yah

Traditional

3. Someone's singin', Lord, Kum-bah-yah. . .
4. Someone's cryin', Lord, Kum-bah-yah. . .
5. Someone's dancin', Lord, Kum-bah-yah. . .
6. Someone's shoutin', Lord, Kum-bah-yah. . .

La Cucaracha

TRADITIONAL MEXICAN

Bright Rhumba

Listen To The Mocking Bird

Words by SEPTIMUS WINNER
Music by RICHARD MILBURN

La Paloma

By SEBASTIÁN YRADIER

Little Brown Jug

Words and Music by
JOSEPH E. WINNER

I love can-dy, I love cake man-y good things are mine to take.

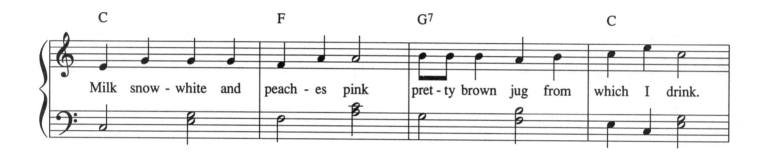

Milk snow-white and peach-es pink pret-ty brown jug from which I drink.

Ho, ho, ho, you and me, lit-tle brown jug how I love thee!

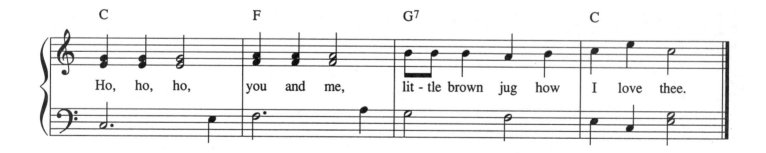

Ho, ho, ho, you and me, lit-tle brown jug how I love thee.

2. My wife and I lived all alone
in a little log hut we called our own,
She loved gin and I loved rum,
I tell you what, we'd lots of fun!

3. 'Tis you who makes my friend my foes,
'Tis you who makes me wear old clothes,
Here you are so near my nose,
So tip her up and down she goes!

Loch Lomond

Traditional Scottish

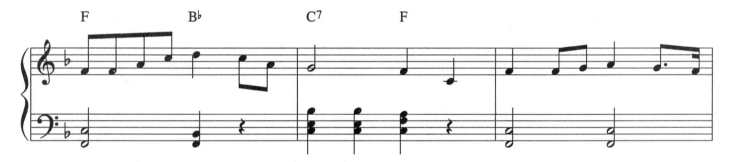

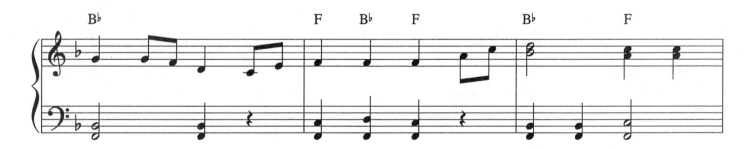

London Bridge

TRADITIONAL ENGLISH

1. Lon - don Bridge is fall - ing down, fall - ing down, fall - ing down,
3. Build it up with sil - ver and gold, sil - ver and gold, sil - ver and gold,

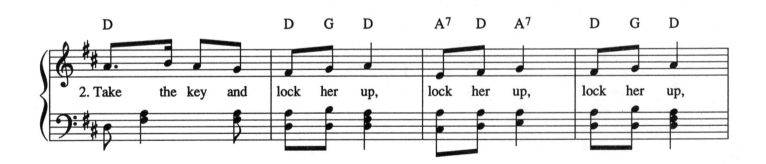

Lon - don Bridge is fall - ing down, My fair la - dy - O.
Build it up with sil - ver and gold,

2. Take the key and lock her up, lock her up, lock her up,

Take the key and lock her up, My fair la - dy - O

Looby Loo

TRADITIONAL

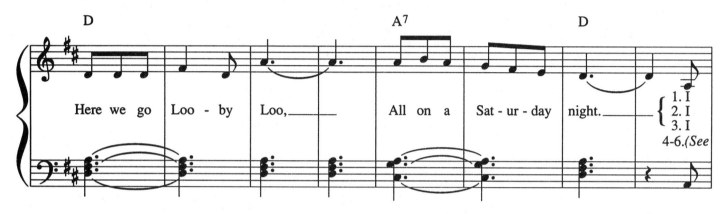

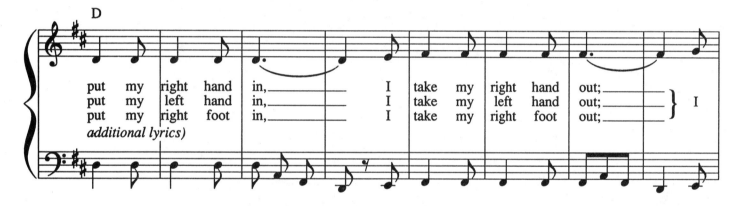

4. I put my left foot in,
   I take my left foot out;
   I give my left foot...

5. I put my big head in,
   I take my big head out;
   I give my big head...

6. I put my whole self in,
   I put my whole self out;
   I give my whole self...

Long, Long Ago

Words and Music by
THOMAS HAYNES BAYLY

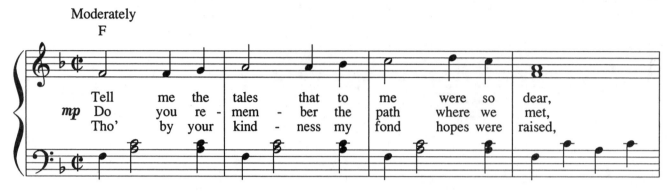

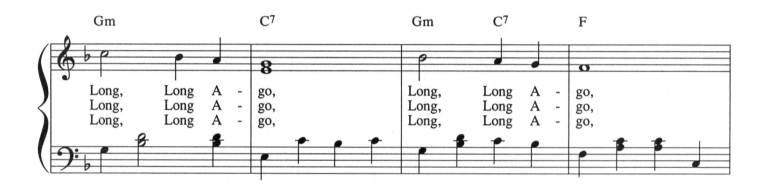

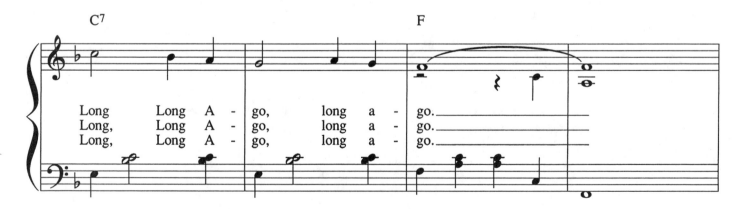

Gm   C7   F

Now   you   are   come,   all   my   grief   is   re - moved;
Then   to   all   oth - ers   my   smile   you   pre - ferred;
But   by   long   ab - cense your   truth   has   been   tried;

Gm   C7   F

Let   me   for - get   that   so   long   you   have   rov'd.
Love,   when   you   spoke,   gave   a   charm   to   each   word.
Still,   to   your   ac - cents, I   lis - ten   with   pride.

F

Let   me   be - lieve   that   you   love   as   you   loved,
Still   my   heart   treas - ures   the   praise - es   I   heard,
Blest   as   I   was   when   I   sat   at   your   side

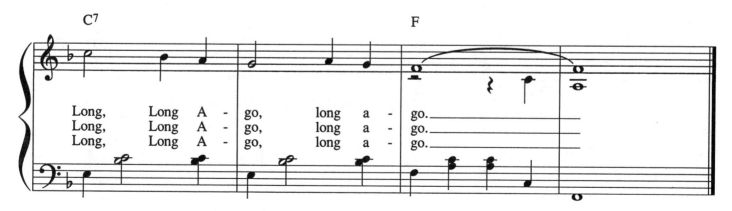

C7   F

Long,   Long   A - go,   long   a - go._____
Long,   Long   A - go,   long   a - go._____
Long,   Long   A - go,   long   a - go._____

March Of The Three Kings

By GEORGES BIZET

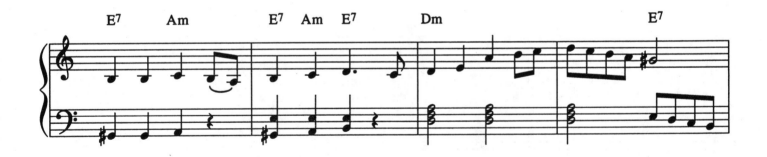

March Slav

By Peter Ilyich Tchaikovsky

Moderate march tempo

Marianne

TRADITIONAL

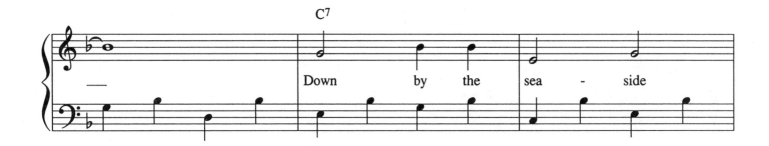

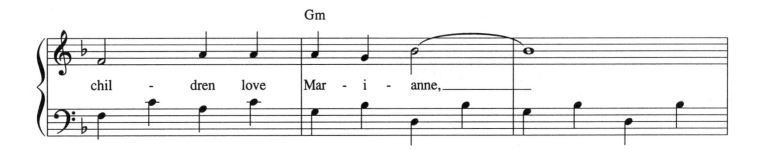

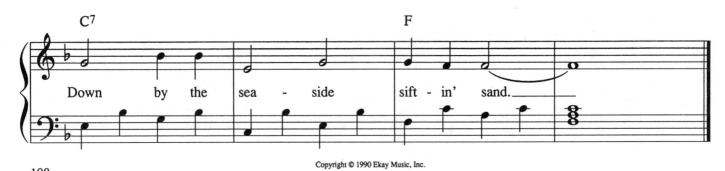

The Marine's Hymn

Words Anonymous
Music based on theme by Jacques Offenbach

Merry Widow Waltz

By Franz Lehar

Michael, Row The Boat Ashore

TRADITIONAL

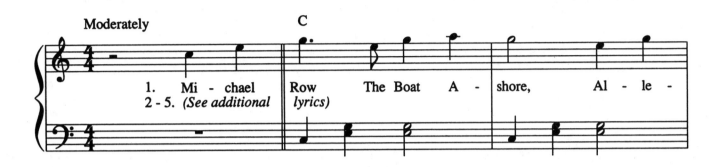

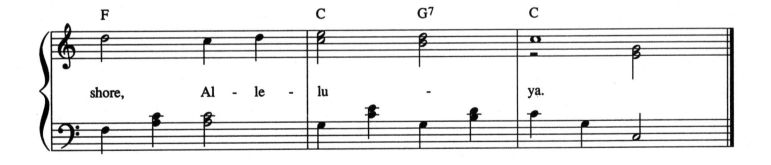

2. Sister, help to trim the sail. . .

3. Michael's boat is a gospel boat. . .

4. Jordan's River is chilly and cold. . .
Chills the body but warms the soul. . .

5. Jordan's River is deep and wide. . .
Meet my mother on the other side. . .

Mexican Hat Dance

TRADITIONAL MEXICAN

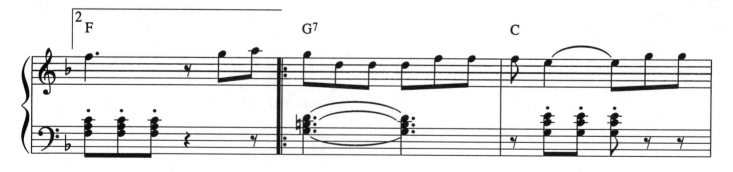

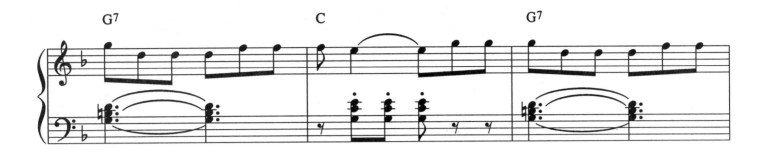

113

Midnight Special

TRADITIONAL

Moderately

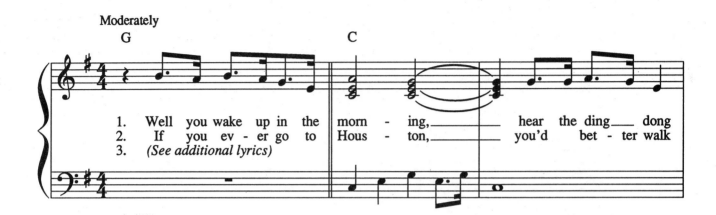

1. Well you wake up in the morn - ing, hear the ding dong
2. If you ev - er go to Hous - ton, you'd bet - ter walk
3. *(See additional lyrics)*

ring, You go march - ing to the ta - ble,
right, And you bet - ter not stag - ger,

see the same damn thing. Well, it's on - ly one
and you bet - ter not fight. 'Cause the sher - iff will ar-

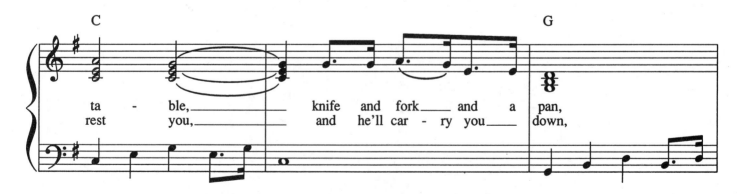

ta - ble, knife and fork and a pan,
rest you, and he'll car - ry you down,

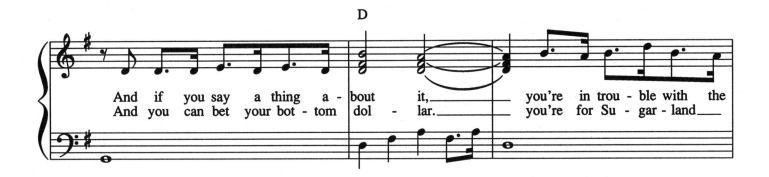

And if you say a thing a-bout it,_____ you're in trou-ble with the
And you can bet your bot-tom dol-lar._____ you're for Su-gar-land_____

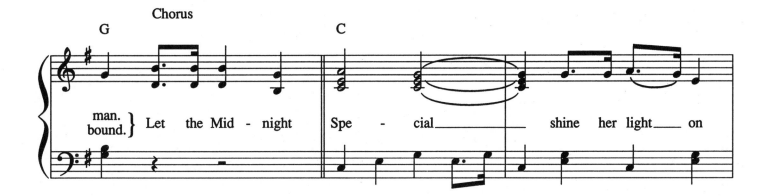

Chorus

man.
bound. } Let the Mid-night Spe-cial_____ shine her light____ on

me, Let the Mid-night Spe-cial_____

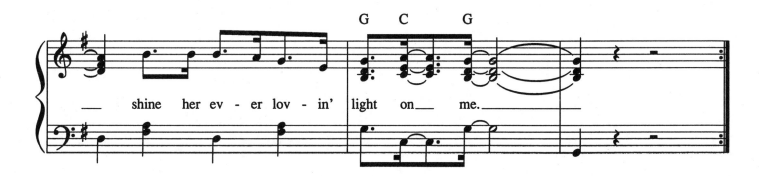

____ shine her ev-er lov-in' light on____ me._____

3. Lord, Thelma said she loved me, but I believe she told a lie,
'Cause she hasn't been to see me since last July.
She brought me little coffee, she brought me little tea,
She brought me nearly everything but the jail house key.

Minuet

By J. S. Bach

Moderately

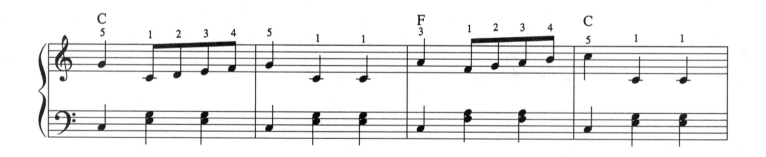

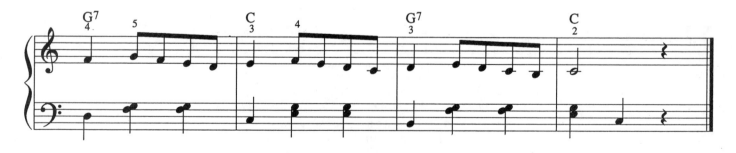

Musetta's Waltz

By GIACOMO PUCCINI

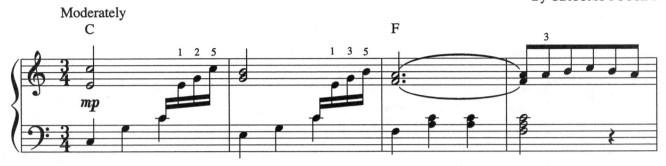

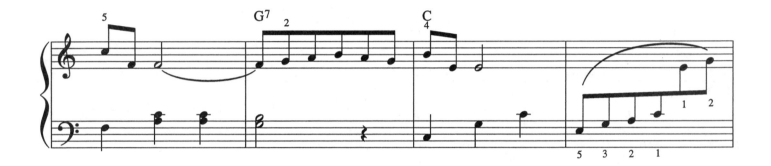

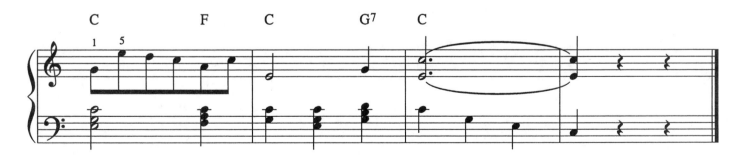

Minuet In G

By Ludwig van Beethoven

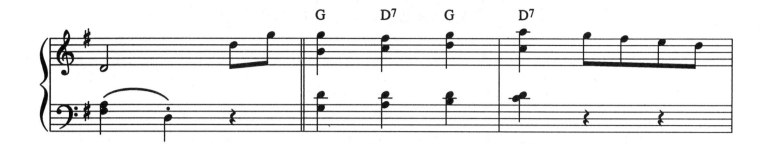

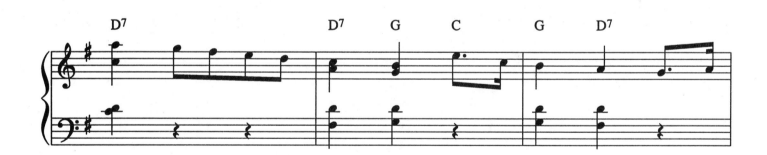

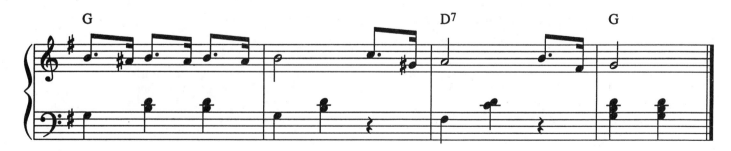

My Darling Clementine

Words and Music by
PERCY MONTROSE

2. Light she was and, like a fairy,
   And her shoes were number nine,
   Herring boxes, without topses,
   Sandals were for Clementine.
   Chorus

3. Drove she ducklings to the water,
   Every morning just at nine,
   Stubbed her toe upon a splinter,
   Fell into the foaming brine.
   Chorus

4. Ruby lips above the water
   Blowing bubbles soft and fine,
   But alas I was no swimmer,
   So I lost my Clementine.
   Chorus

5. There's a churchyard, on the hillside,
   Where the flowers grow and twine,
   There grow roses, 'mongst the posies,
   Fertilized by Clementine.
   Chorus

My Old Kentucky Home

Words and Music by
STEPHEN FOSTER

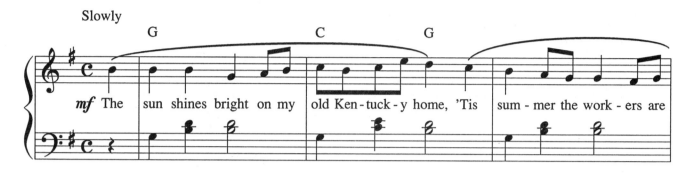

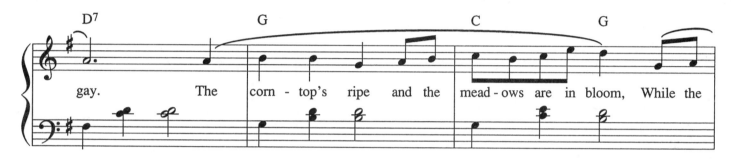

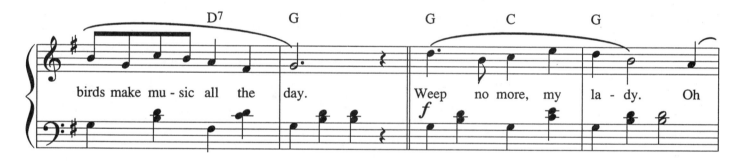

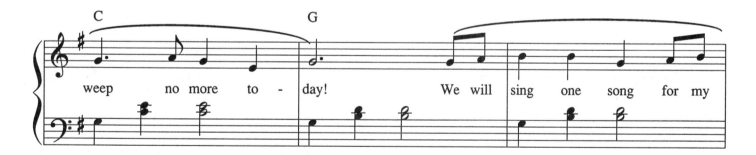

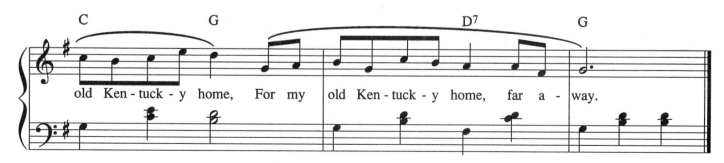

Oh, Susanna

Words and Music by
STEPHEN FOSTER

3. I had a dream the other night
   When everything was still.
   I thought I saw Susanna
   A-coming down the hill.

4. The buckwheat cake was in her mouth,
   The tear was in her eye,
   Say I, "I'm coming from the South,
   Susanna, don't you cry."

Oh! Them Golden Slippers

Words and Music by
JAMES A. BLAND

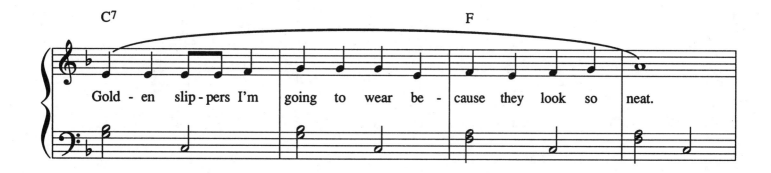

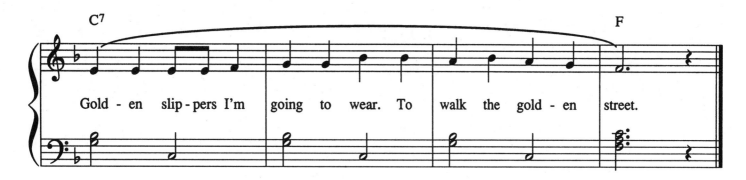

Oh Where, Oh Where Has My Little Dog Gone?

Words by SEPTIMUS WINNER
Music TRADITIONAL ENGLISH

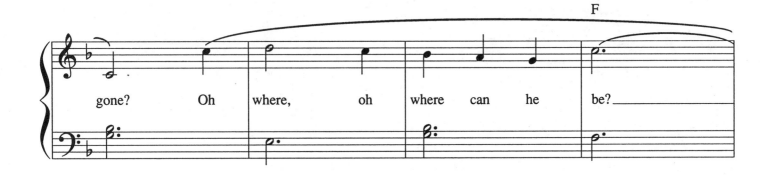

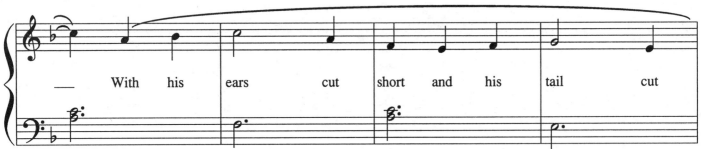

The Old Folks at Home

Words and Music by
STEPHEN FOSTER

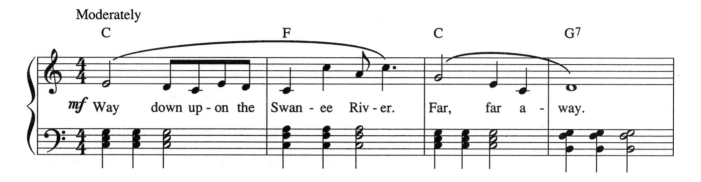

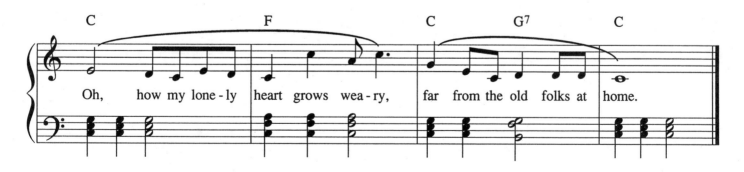

125

Old MacDonald

Words by THOMAS D'URFEY
Music TRADITIONAL

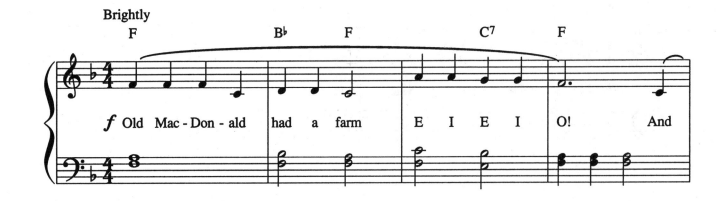

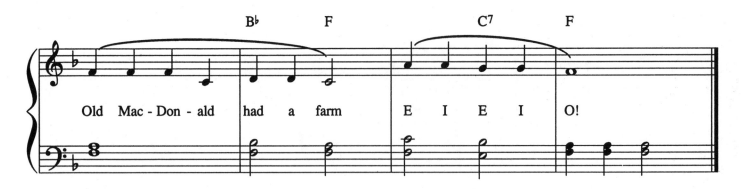

On Top of Old Smokey

TRADITIONAL

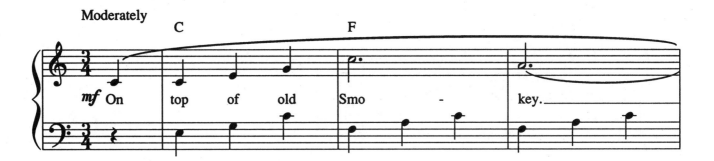

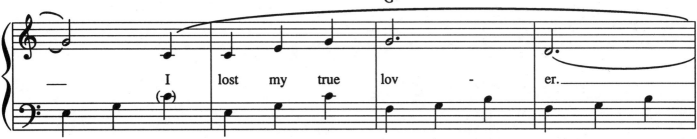

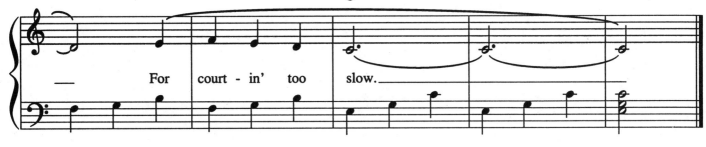

O Sole Mio

By Edoardo Di Capua

Moderately

Over the River and Through the Woods

TRADITIONAL

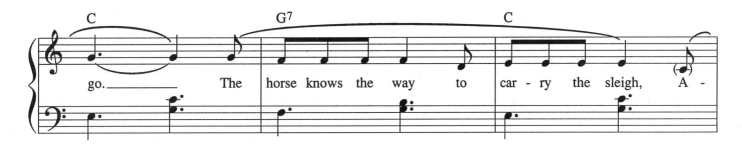

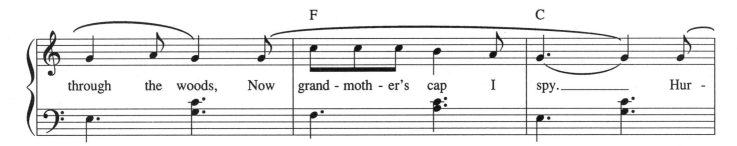

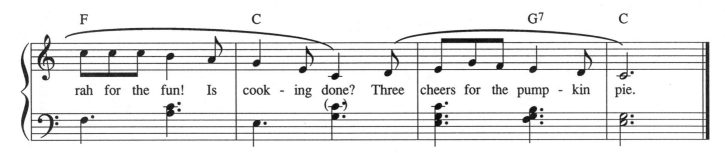

Pat-a-pan

Words and Music by
BERNARD DE LA MONNOYE

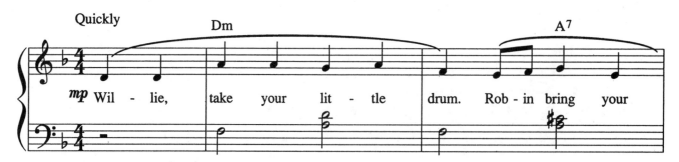

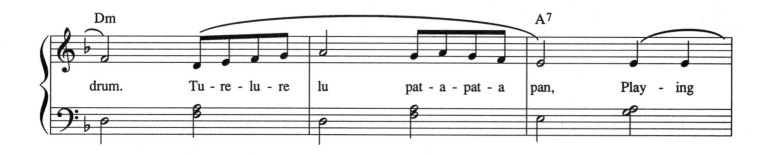

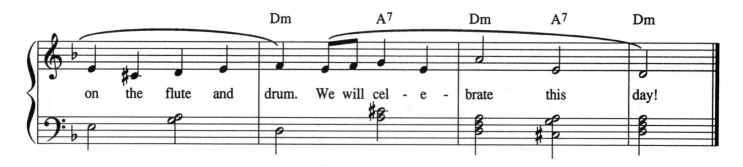

Polly Wolly Doodle

TRADITIONAL

Brightly

mf Oh, I went down South for to see my Sal Sing-ing Pol-ly-Wol-ly Doo-dle all the

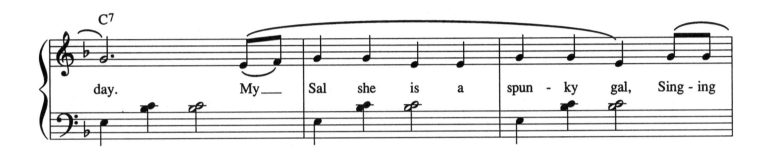

day. My Sal she is a spun-ky gal, Sing-ing

Pol-ly-Wol-ly Doo-dle all the day. Fare thee well, Fare thee

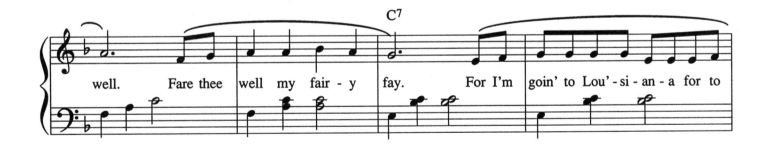

well. Fare thee well my fair-y fay. For I'm goin' to Lou'-si-an-a for to

see my Su-zi-an-a, sing-ing Pol-ly Wol-ly Doo-dle all the day.

Prelude

By Frédéric Chopin

Moderately

Put Your Arms Around Me, Honey

Words by Junie McCree
Music by Albert Von Tilzer

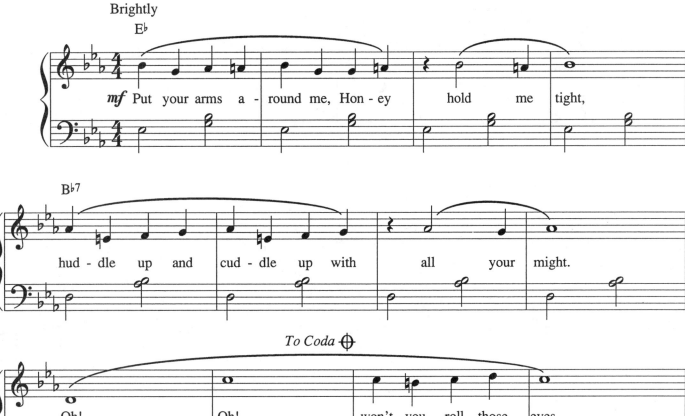

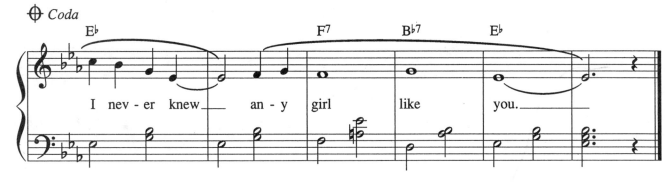

Red River Valley

ANONYMOUS

Moderately

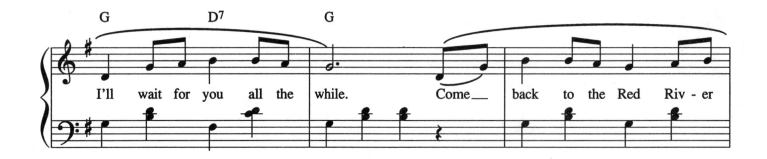

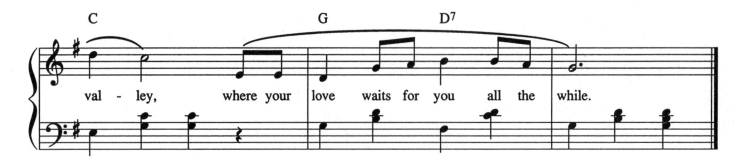

Rock of Ages

Words by AUGUSTUS MONTAGUE TOPLADY
Music by THOMAS HASTINGS

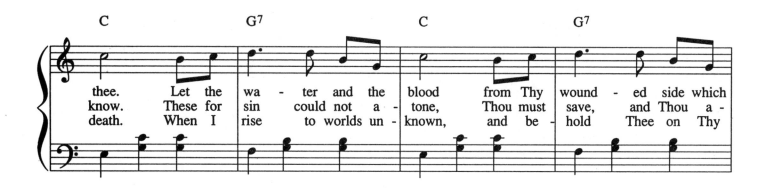

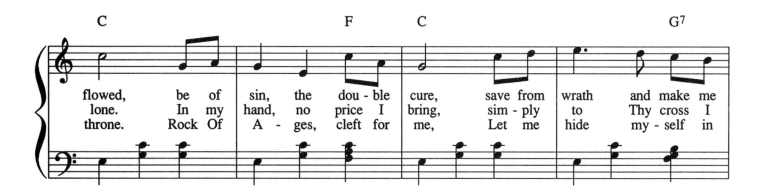

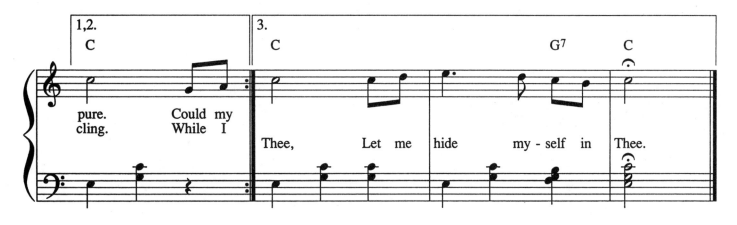

The Rock Island Line

TRADITIONAL

Quickly

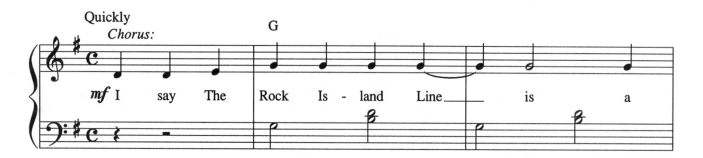

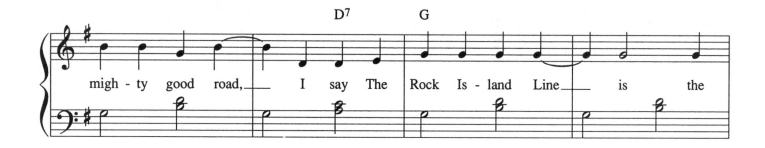

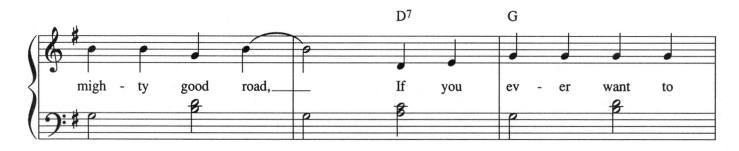

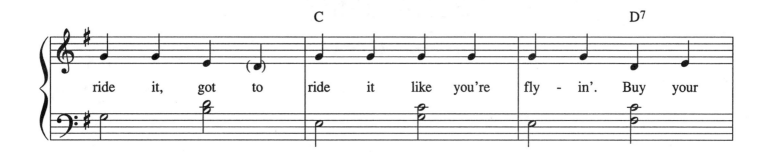

C   **D⁷**

ride it, got to ride it like you're fly - in'. Buy your

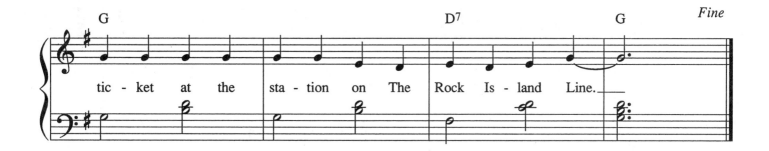

G   **D⁷**   **G**   *Fine*

tic - ket at the sta - tion on The Rock Is - land Line.

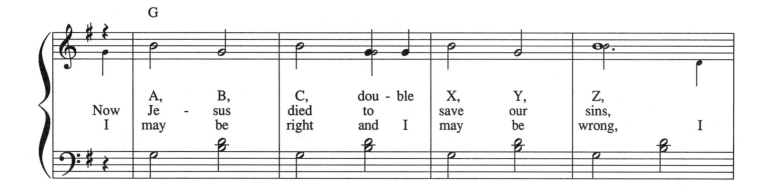

G

Now A, B, C, dou - ble X, Y, Z,

I Je - sus died right to and I save our be sins, wrong, I

D.C. al Fine
(3x)

D⁷   **G**

Cat's in the cup - board, but he can't see me.

Glo - ry be to God, we're gon - na need Him a - gain.

know you're gon - na miss me when I am gone.

Rondeau
(Mouret)

By Jean-Joseph Mouret

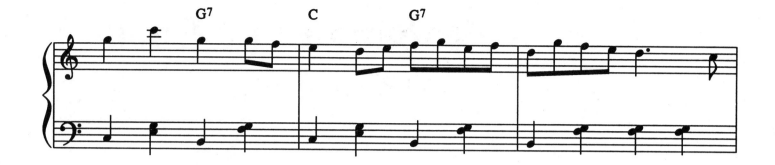

Fine

D.C. al Fine

Row, Row, Row Your Boat

ANONYMOUS

Brightly

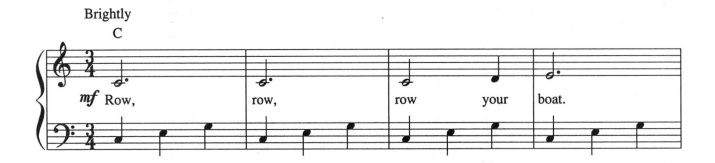

Row, row, row your boat.

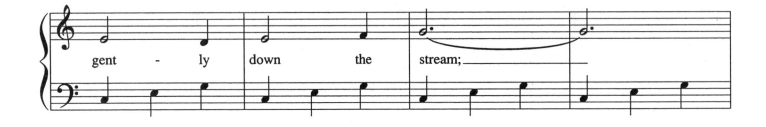

gent - ly down the stream;

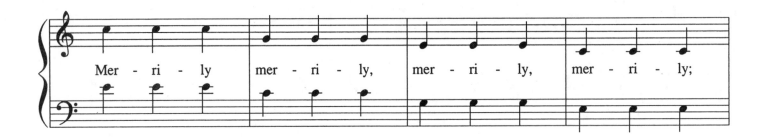

Mer - ri - ly mer - ri - ly, mer - ri - ly, mer - ri - ly;

life is but a dream.

Shall We Gather at the River

Words and Music by
ROBERT LOWRY

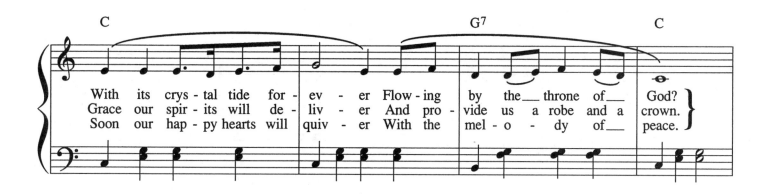

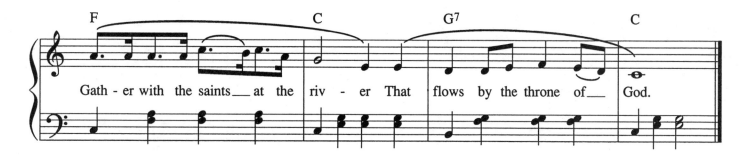

Santa Lucia

By Teodoro Cottrau

She'll Be Comin' 'Round the Mountain

TRADITIONAL

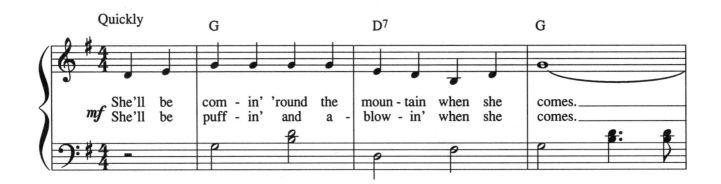

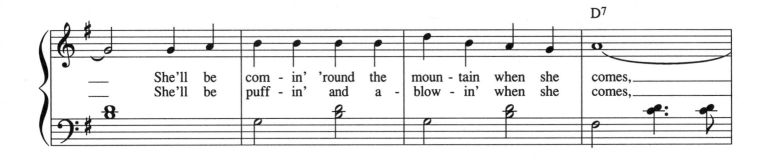

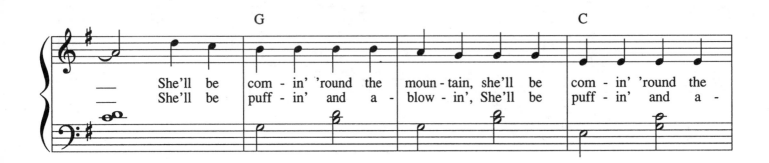

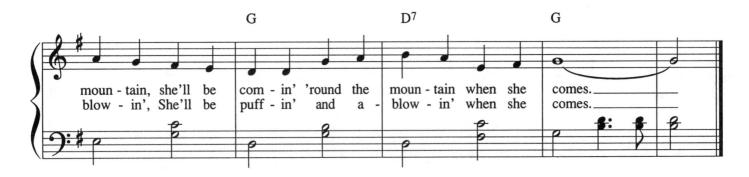

Shenandoah

TRADITIONAL

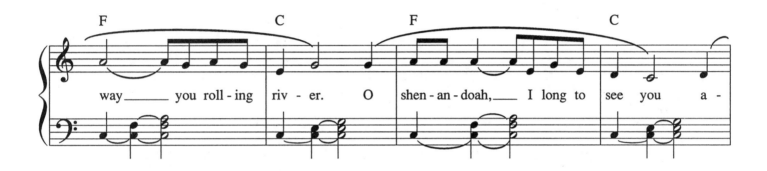

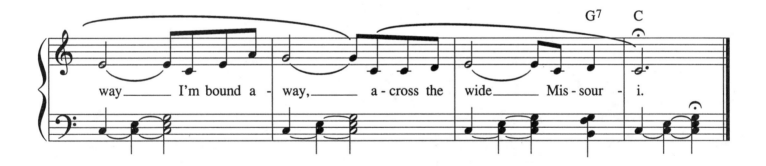

2. O Shenandoah, I love your daughter,
   Away, you rolling river,
   For her I've crossed the rolling water,
   Away, I'm bound away,
   Across the wide Missouri.

3. The trader loved this Indian maiden,
   Away, you rolling river,
   With presents his canoe was laden,
   Away I'm bound away,
   Across the wide Missouri.

4. O Shenandoah, I'm bound to leave you,
   Away, you rolling river,
   O Shenandoah, I'll not deceive you.
   Away, I'm bound away,
   Across the wide Missouri.

5. O Shenandoah, I long to hear you,
   Away, you rolling river,
   O Shenandoah, I long to hear you.
   Away, I'm bound away,
   Across the wide Missouri.

Shortnin' Bread

TRADITIONAL

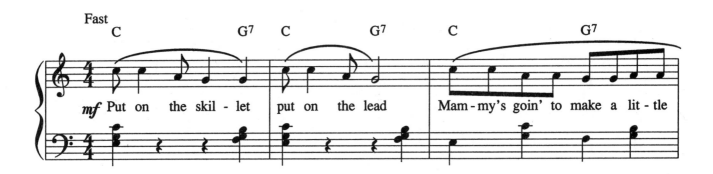

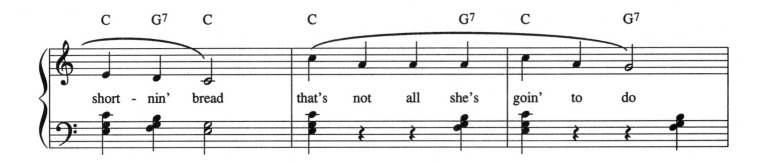

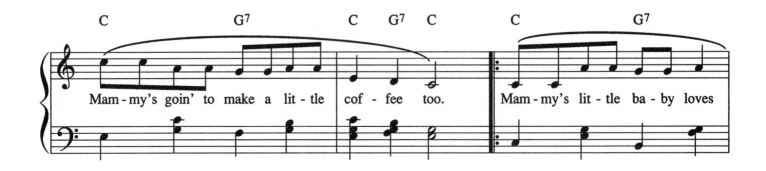

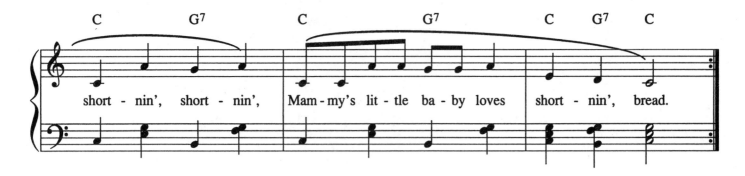

146

Silent Night

Words by JOSEPH MOHR
English translation by JOHN F. YOUNG
Music by FRANZ GRÜBER

Gently

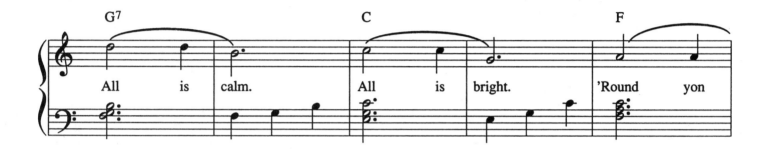

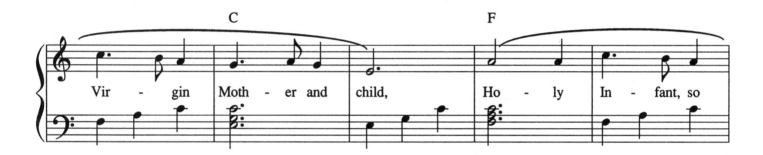

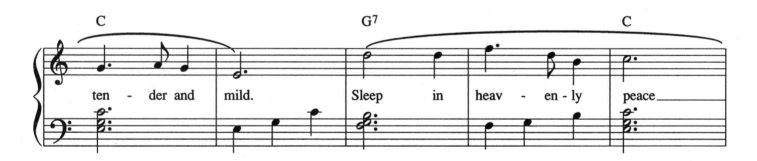

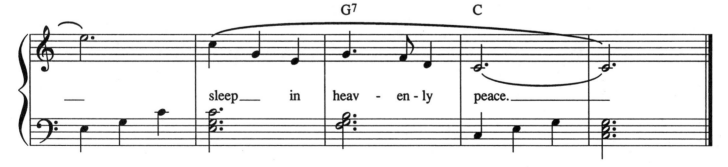

The Sidewalks of New York
(East Side, West Side)

Words and Music by
CHARLES B. LAWLOR
and JAMES W. BLAKE

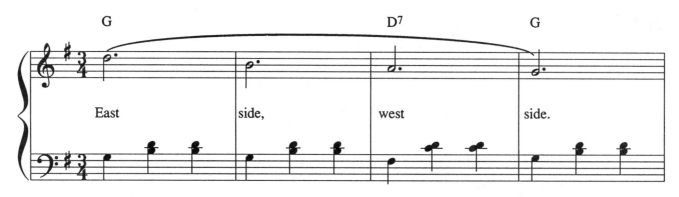

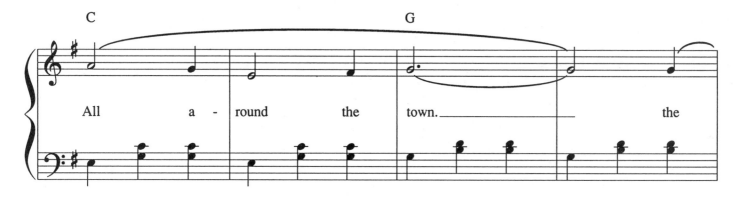

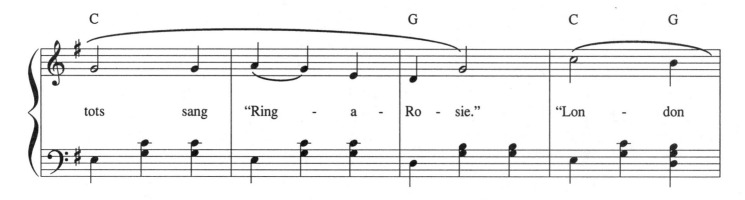

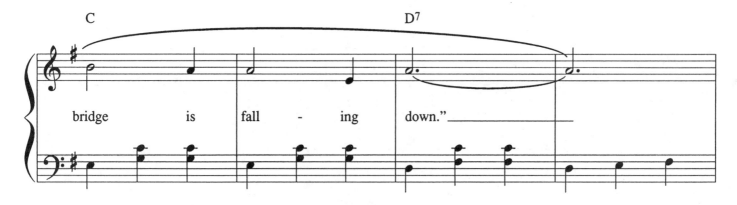

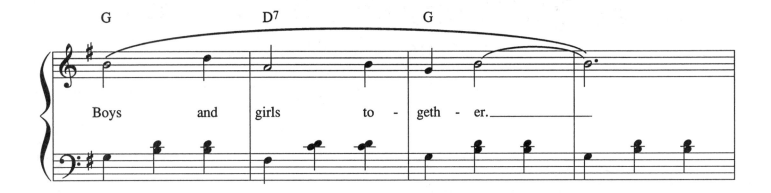

Boys and girls to - geth - er.

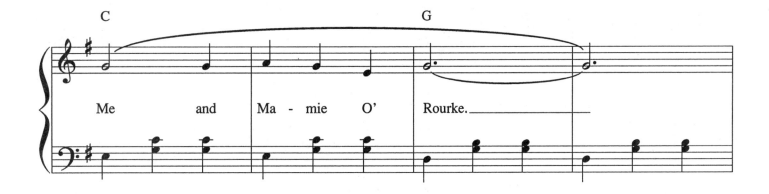

Me and Ma - mie O' Rourke.

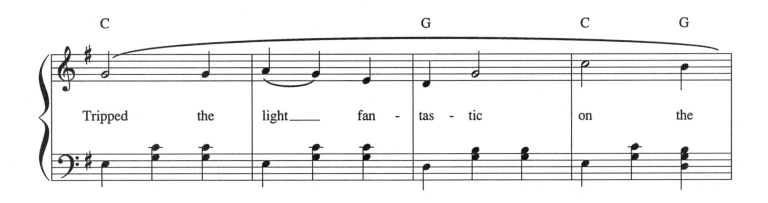

Tripped the light____ fan - tas - tic on the

side - walks of New York.____

149

Silver Threads Among the Gold

Words by EBEN E. REXFORD
Music by HART PEASE DANKS

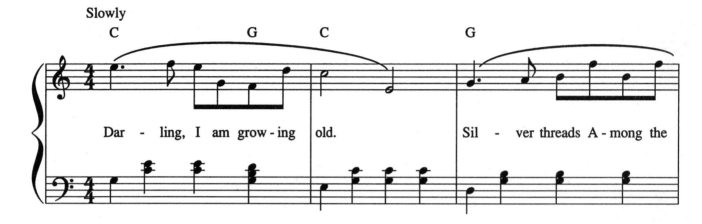

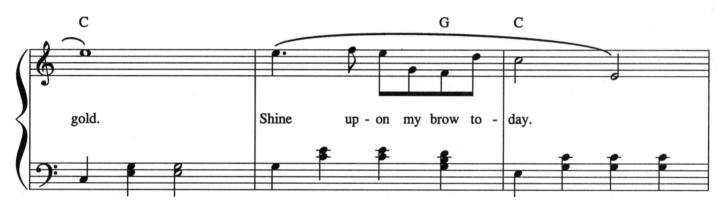

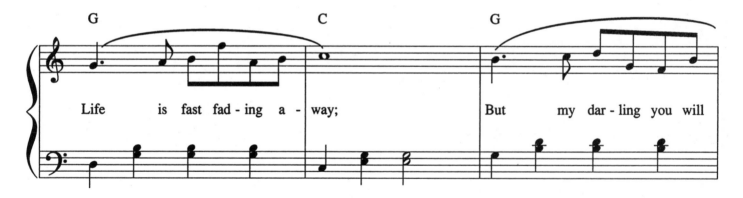

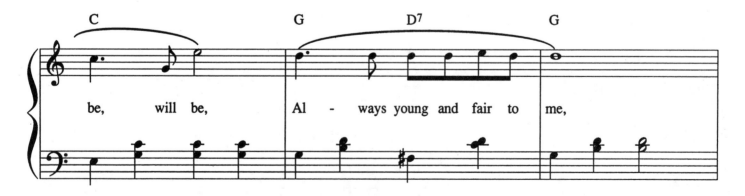

yea, my dar - ling you will be   Al - ways young and fair to

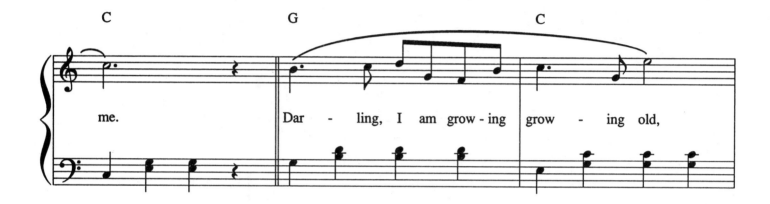

me.   Dar - ling, I am grow - ing grow - ing old,

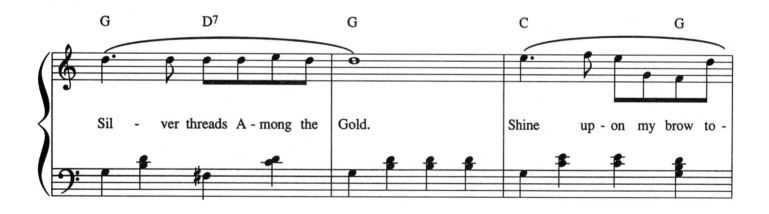

Sil - ver threads A - mong the Gold.   Shine up - on my brow to -

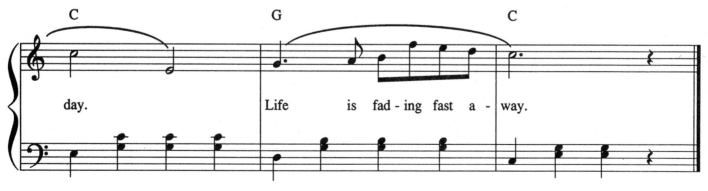

day.   Life is fad - ing fast a - way.

Skip to My Lou

TRADITIONAL

152

Sometimes I Feel Like a Motherless Child

TRADITIONAL

Sonata (Themes)

By WOLFGANG A. MOZART

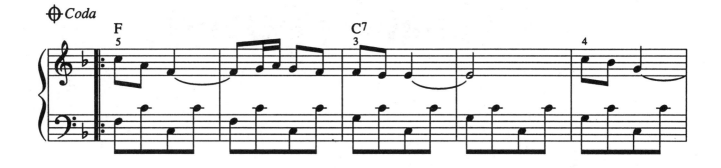

Song of the Volga Boatmen

TRADITIONAL RUSSIAN

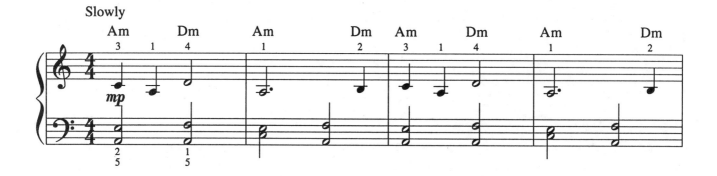

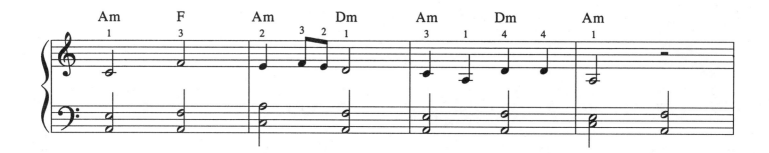

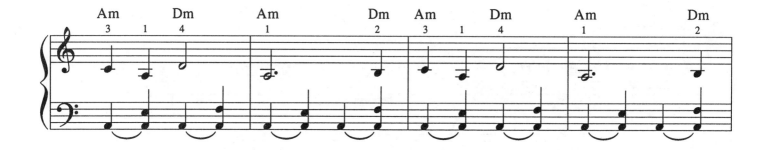

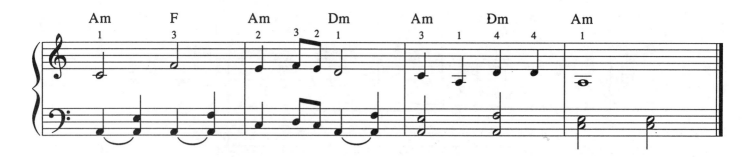

The Streets of Laredo

ANONYMOUS

2. "I see by your outfit that you are a cowboy,"
   These words he did say as I proudly stepped by,
   "Come sit down beside me and hear my sad story,
   Got shot in the breast and I know I must die."

3. "Twas once in the saddle I used to go dashing,
   'Twas once in the saddle I used to go gay;
   'Twas first to drinkin', and then to card-playing,
   Got shot in the breast and I'm dying today."

4. "Let six jolly cowboys come carry my coffin,
   Let six pretty gals come carry my pall;
   Throw bunches of roses all over my coffin,
   Throw roses to deaden the clods as they fall.

5. "Oh, beat the drum slowly, and play the fife lowly,
   And play the dead march as you carry me along,
   Take me to the green valley and lay the earth o'er me,
   For I'm a poor cowboy and I know I've done wrong."

6. Oh we beat the drum slowly and we played the fife lowly,
   And bitterly wept as we carried him along,
   For we all loved our comrade, so brave, young and handsome.
   Wrapped in white linen as cold as the clay.

The Star Spangled Banner

Words by FRANCIS SCOTT KEY
Music by JOHN STAFFORD SMITH

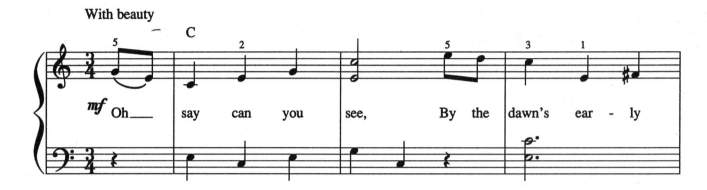

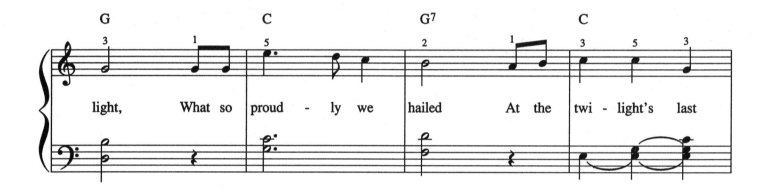

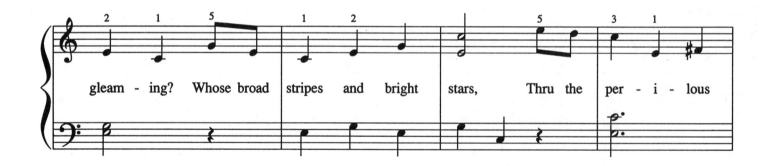

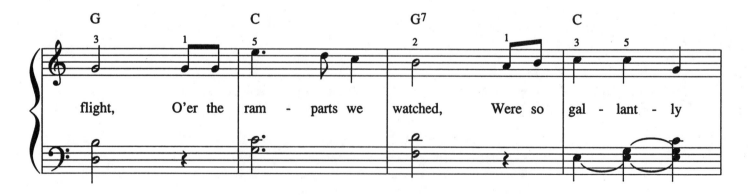

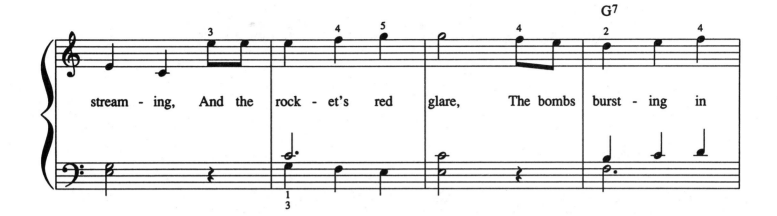

stream - ing, And the rock - et's red glare, The bombs burst - ing in

air, Gave proof thru the night that our flag was still

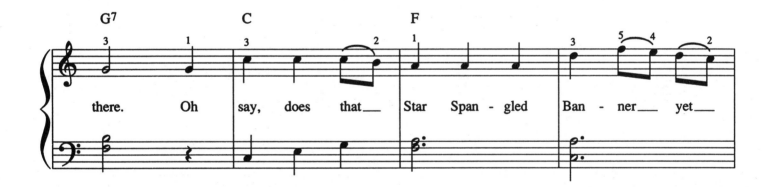

there. Oh say, does that___ Star Span - gled Ban - ner___ yet___

wave___ O'er the land___ of the free And the home of the brave?

St. James Infirmary

Words and Music by
JOE PRIMROSE

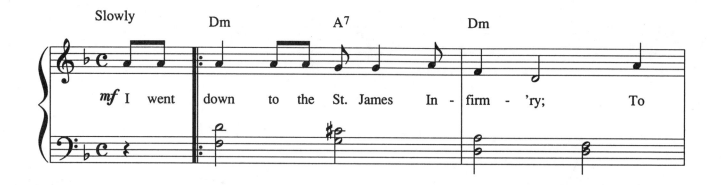

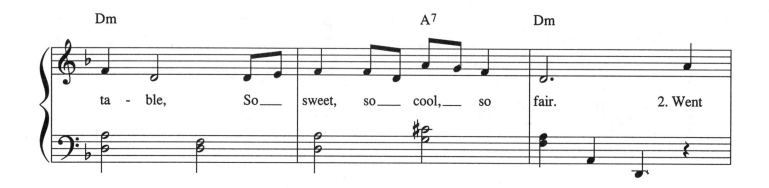

160

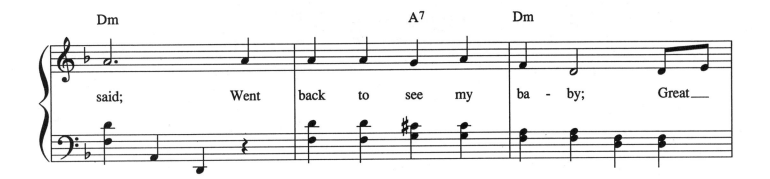

said; Went back to see my ba - by; Great___

God! She was ly - in' there dead. I went blues.

3. I went down to old Joe's barroom,
   On the corner by the square;
   They were servin' the drinks as usual,
   And the usual crowd was there.

4. On my left stood Joe McKennedy,
   His eyes bloodshot red;
   He turned to the crowd around him,
   These are the words he said:

5. Let her go, let her go, God bless her;
   Wherever she may be;
   She may search this wide world over
   She'll never find a man like me.

6. Oh, when I die, please bury me
   In my high-top Stetson hat;
   Put a gold piece on my watch chain
   So they'll know I died standin' pat.

7. Get six gamblers to carry my coffin,
   Six chorus girls to sing my song,
   Put a jazz band on my tail gate
   To raise Hell as we go along.

8. Now that's the end of my story;
   Let's have another round of booze;
   And if anyone should ask you, just tell them
   I've got The St. James Infirmary blues.

Sweet Molly Malone

TRADITIONAL

Moderately

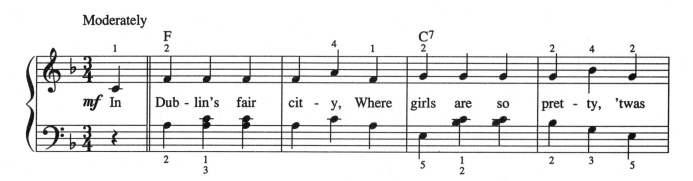

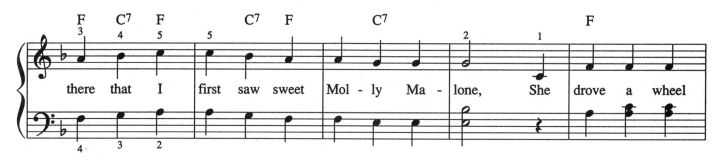

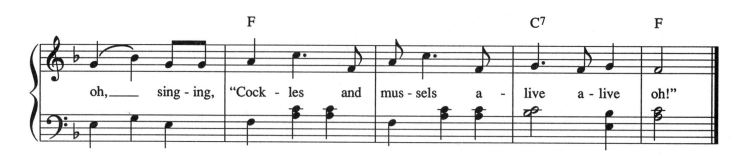

Swing Low, Sweet Chariot

TRADITIONAL

163

Ta-Ra-Ra Boom-Der-É

Words and Music by
HENRY J. SAYERS

A sweet tux-e-do girl you see, Queen of swell so-ci-e-ty,
blush-ing bud of in-no-cence, Pa-pa says at big ex-pense,

Fond of fun as fond can be, When it's on the strict Q. T. I'm
Old maids say I have no sense, Boys de-clare I'm just im-mense, Be-

not too young. I'm not too old, Not too tim-id, Not too bold,
fore my song I do con-clude, I want it strict-ly un-der-stood, Tho'

Just the kind you'd like to hold Just the kind for sport I'm told. }
fond of fun, I'm nev-er rude, Tho' not too bad I'm not too good. }

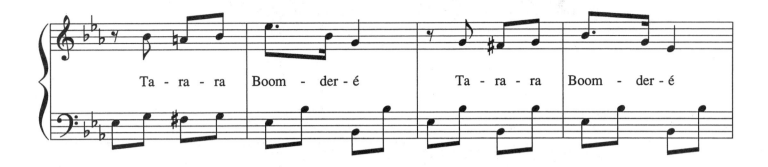

Ta - ra - ra Boom - der - é Ta - ra - ra Boom - der - é

Ta - ra - ra Boom - der - é Ta - ra - ra Boom - der - é Ta - ra - ra

Boom - der - é Ta - ra - ra Boom - der - é Ta - ra - ra Boom - der - é

Ta - ra - ra Boom - der - é. I'm a Ta - ra - ra - Boom - der - é.

There Is a Tavern in the Town

Anonymous

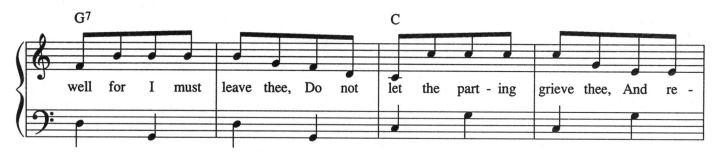

mem - ber that the best of friends must part, must part. A -

dieu, a - dieu kind friends a - dieu._____ I

can no long - er stay with you, Stay with you,___ I'll___

hang my harp on a weep - ing will - ow tree, And

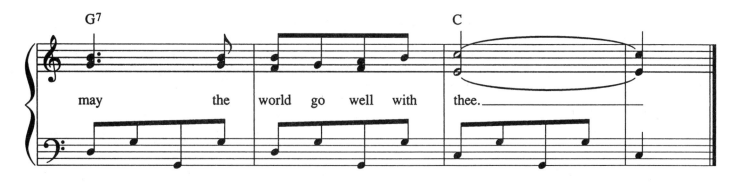

may the world go well with thee._____

This Old Man

ANONYMOUS

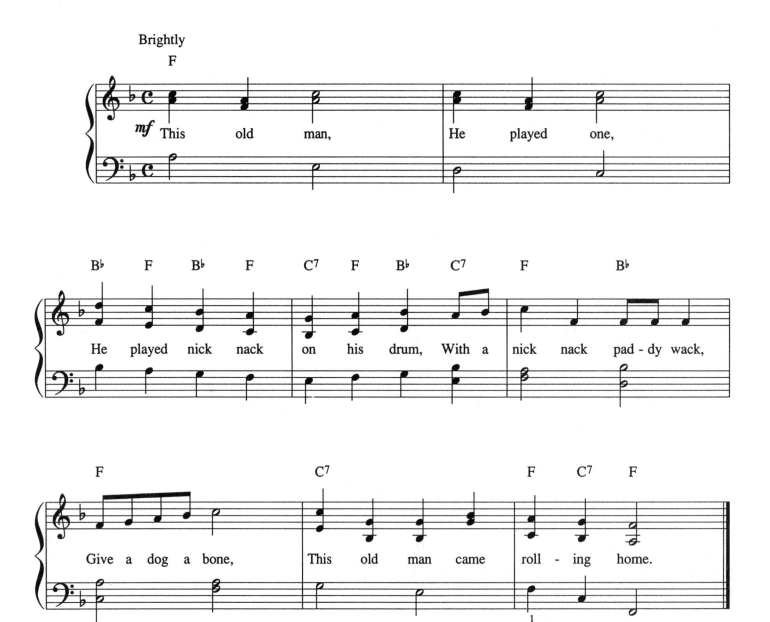

2. This old man, he played two, he played nick nack on his shoe,
   With a nick nack, paddy wack, give a dog a bone, This old man came rolling home.

3. This old man, he played three, he played nick nack on his knee,
   With a nick nack, etc...

4. This old man, he played four, he played nick nack on his door,
   With a nick nack, etc...

5. This old man, he played five, he played nick nack on the drive,
   With a nick nack, etc...

This Train

TRADITIONAL

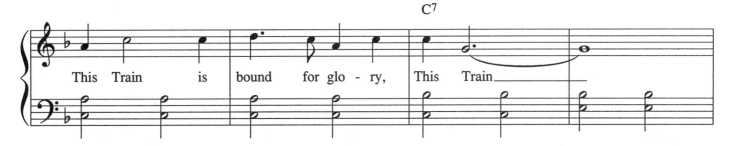

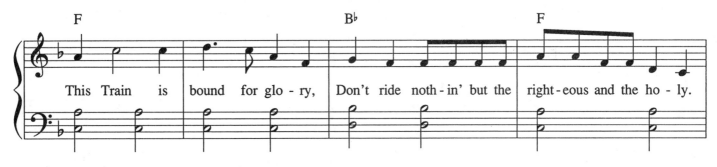

2. This Train don't carry no gamblers, *(3 times)*
   No hypocrites, no midnight ramblers,
   This Train is bound for glory, This Train.

3. This Train is built for speed now, *(3 times)*
   Fastest train you ever did see,
   This Train is bound for glory, This Train.

4. This Train don't carry no liars, *(3 times)*
   No hypocrites and no high flyers,
   This Train is bound for glory, This Train.

5. This Train you don't pay no transportation, *(3 times)*
   No Jim Crow and no discrimination,
   This Train is bound for glory, This Train.

6. This Train don't carry no rustlers, *(3 times)*
   Sidestreet walkers, two-bit hustlers,
   This Train is bound for glory, This Train.

Three Blind Mice

ANONYMOUS

Moderately

Three blind mice, Three blind mice,

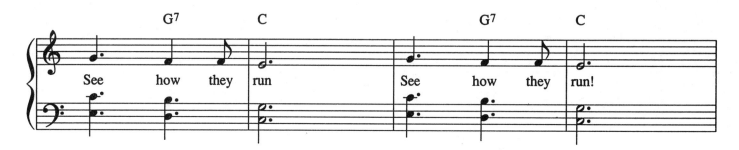

See how they run See how they run!

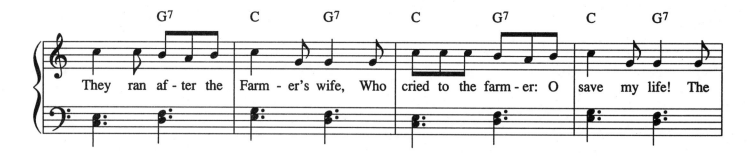

They ran af - ter the Farm - er's wife, Who cried to the farm - er: O save my life! The

farm - er re - plied: They are real - ly quite nice, Oh the three blind mice

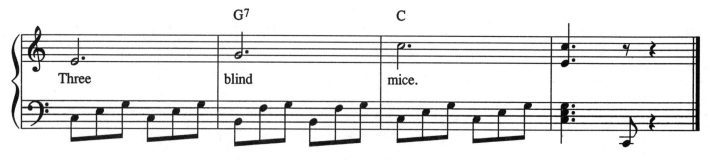

Three blind mice.

Turkey in the Straw

ANONYMOUS

Liltingly

As__ I was a-go-ing on__ down the road, With a ti-red team__ and a

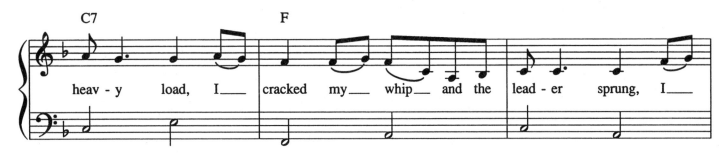

heav-y load, I__ cracked my__ whip__ and the lead-er sprung, I__

Chorus:

says day day__ to the wa-gon tongue, Tur-key in the straw haw,__ haw,__ haw,

Tur-key in the hay hay,__ hay,__ hey. Roll 'em up and twist 'em up a

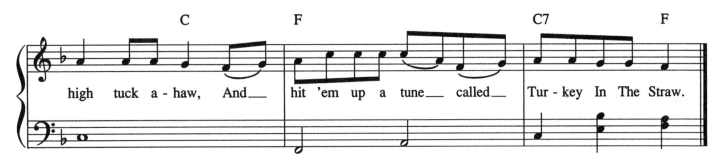

high tuck a-haw, And__ hit 'em up a tune__ called__ Tur-key In The Straw.

Twinkle, Twinkle, Little Star

Words by JANE TAYLOR
TRADITIONAL FRENCH FOLKSONG

Moderately

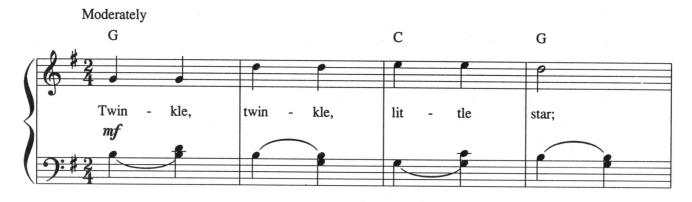

Twin - kle, twin - kle, lit - tle star;

mf

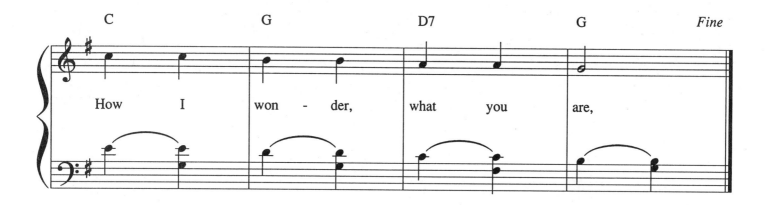

How I won - der, what you are,

Fine

Up a - bove the world so high,

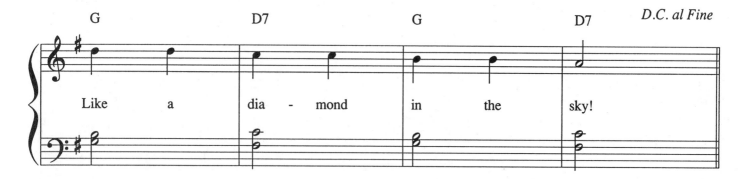

Like a dia - mond in the sky!

D.C. al Fine

Two Guitars

TRADITIONAL RUSSIAN

Moderately slow

Fine

D.C. al Fine

The Wabash Cannonball

TRADITIONAL

Moderately

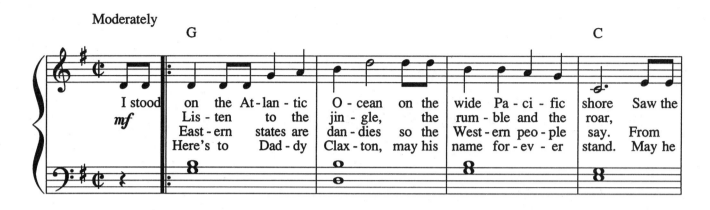

I stood on the At-lan-tic O-cean on the wide Pa-ci-fic shore Saw the
Lis-ten to the jin-gle, the rum-ble and the West-ern peo-ple say. From
East-ern states are dan-dies so the name for-ev-er stand. May he
Here's to Dad-dy Clax-ton, may his

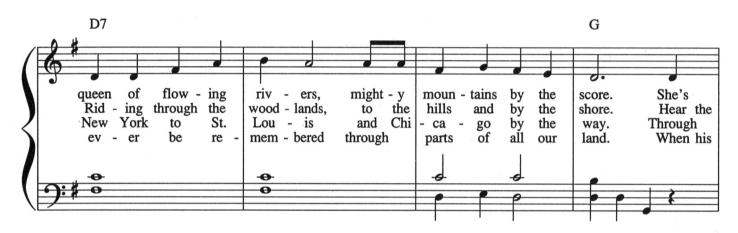

queen of flow-ing riv-ers, might-y moun-tains by the score. She's
Rid-ing through the wood-lands, to the hills and by the shore. Hear the
New York to St. Lou-is and Chi-ca-go by the way. Through
ev-er be re-mem-bered through parts of all our land. When his

long-and she's tall and hand-some yes, she's loved by one and all; she's a
might-y rush of the en-gine hear the lone-some ho-bo squall,
the hills of Min-ne-so-ta where the rip-pling wa-ters fall, no
earth-ly race is o-ver and the cur-tain 'round him fall, we'll

mod-ern com-bi-na-tion called The Wa-bash Can-non-ball.
rid-ing through the jun-gle on The Wa-bash Can-non-ball.
chanc-es can be tak-en on The Wa-bash Can-non-ball.
car-ry him to glo-ry on The Wa-bash Can-non-ball.

1-3.
G

4.
G
ball.

When Johnny Comes Marching Home

Words and Music by
PATRICK SARSFIELD GILMORE

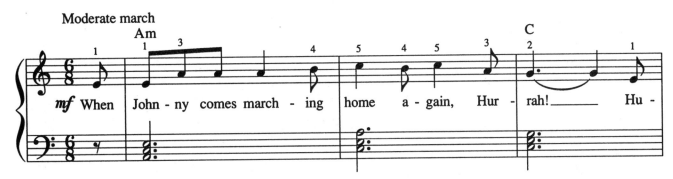

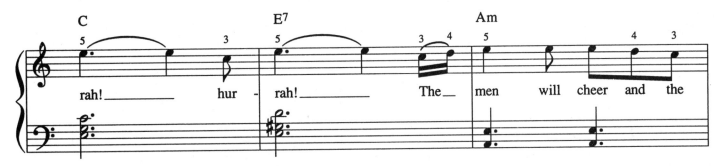

When the Saints Go Marching In

Words by KATHARINE E. PURVIS
Music by JAMES M. BLACK

Moderately bright

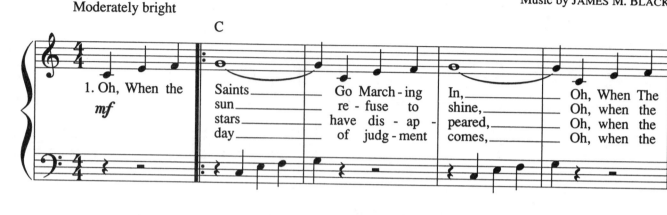

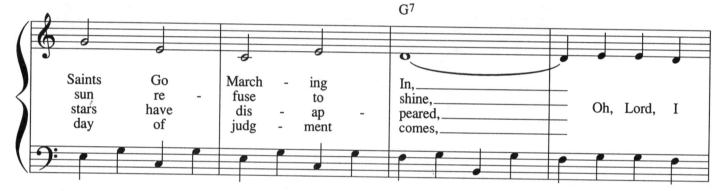

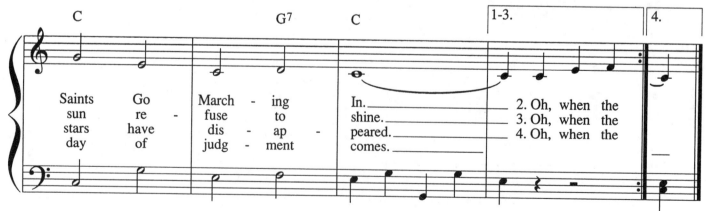

When You and I Were Young, Maggie

Words by George W. Johnson
Music by James Austin Butterfield

Will the Circle Be Unbroken

TRADITIONAL

Yankee Doodle

TRADITIONAL

Brightly

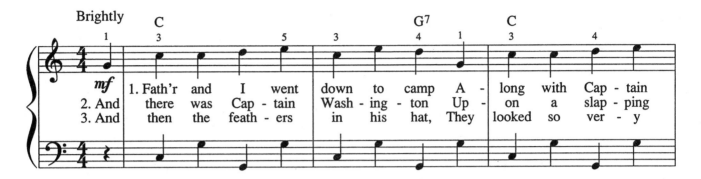

1. Fath'r and I went down to camp A - long with Cap - tain
2. And there was Cap - tain Wash - ing - ton Up - on a slap - ping
3. And then the feath - ers in his hat, They looked so ver - y

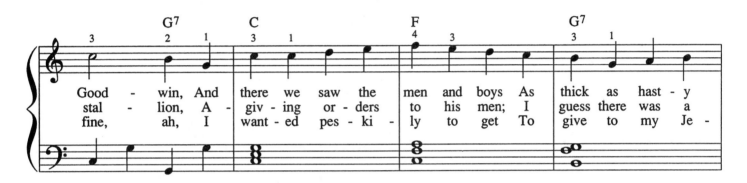

Good - win, And there we saw the men and boys As thick as hast - y
stal - lion, A - giv - ing or - ders to his men; I guess there was a
fine, ah, I want - ed pes - ki - ly to get To give to my Je -

pud - din'. Yan - kee Doo - dle keep it up, Yan - kee Doo - dle
mil - lion.
mi - ma.

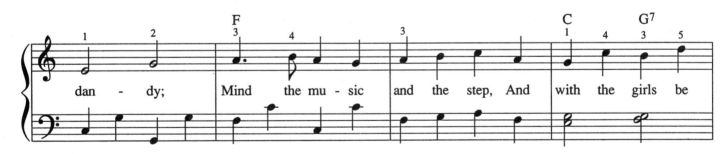

dan - dy; Mind the mu - sic and the step, And with the girls be

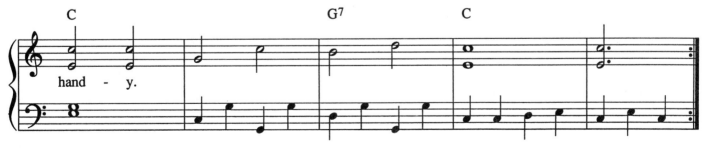

hand - y.

The Yellow Rose of Texas

TRADITIONAL

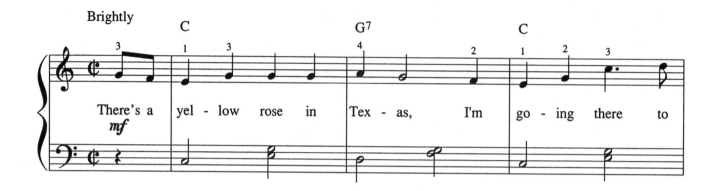

There's a yel - low rose in Tex - as, I'm go - ing there to

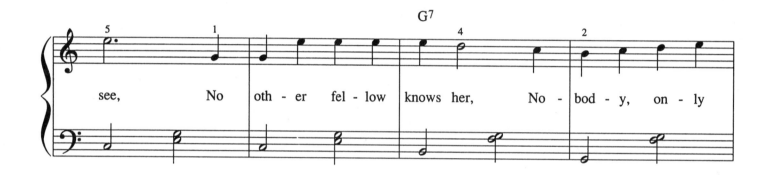

see, No oth - er fel - low knows her, No - bod - y, on - ly

me. She__ cried so when I left her, it like to broke her

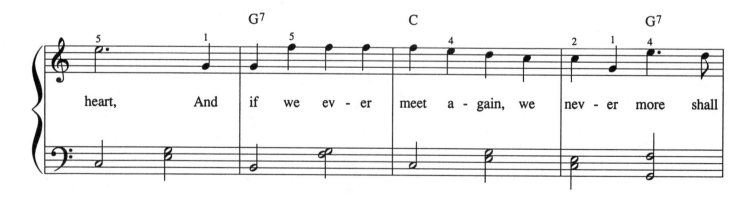

heart, And if we ev - er meet a - gain, we nev - er more shall

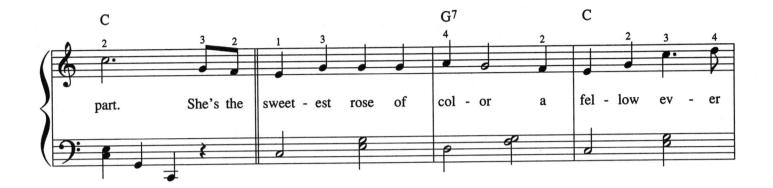

part. She's the sweet - est rose of col - or a fel - low ev - er

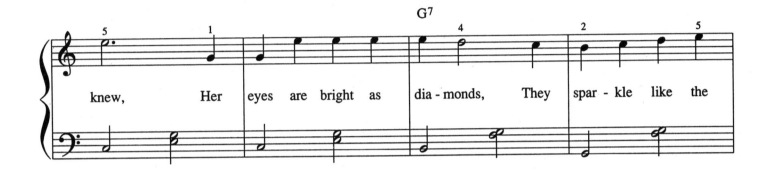

knew, Her eyes are bright as dia - monds, They spar - kle like the

dew. You may talk a - bout your dear - est maids and sing of Ro - sy

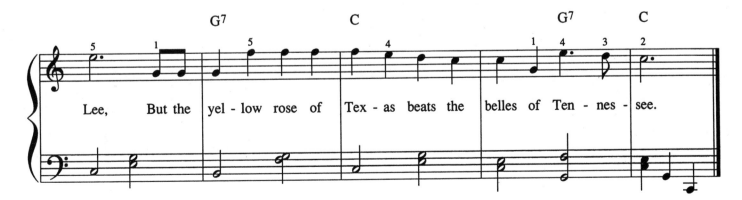

Lee, But the yel - low rose of Tex - as beats the belles of Ten - nes - see.

Zum Gali Gali

TRADITIONAL JEWISH

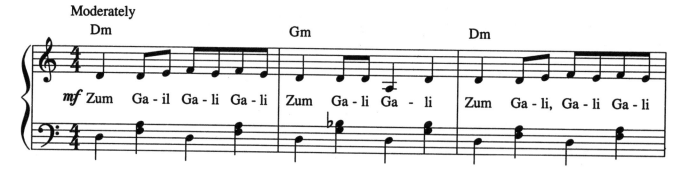

Translation: "The Pioneer is meant for work. Work is meant for the Pioneer."